Small Endearments
Nineteenth-Century Quilts for Children

Small Endearments

Nineteenth-Century
Quilts
for
Children

◆◆◆

SANDI FOX

CHARLES SCRIBNER'S SONS · NEW YORK

This Small Endearment
is for my daughter, Heather

Fox, Sandi.
Small endearments.
Bibliography: p.
Includes index.
1. Children's quilts—United States—History—19th
century—Exhibitions. I. Title.
NK9112.F695 1985   746.9'7'0973   84-23621
ISBN 0-684-18185-1

1 3 5 7 9 11 13 15 17 19 H/C 20 18 16 14 12 10 8 6 4 2

Printed in the United States of America.

CONTENTS

✦✦✦

Acknowledgments   *vii*

INTRODUCTION   *1*

PART I: Images and Imagination

CHAPTER 1:   Reality   7
      Baskets/The Heavens/Flying Geese/
      The Forests/Botanical Observations

CHAPTER 2:   Refinement   37
      Animals/Toys and Games/Literary
      Influences/A Reflection of the Decorative Arts

PART II: Individuals and Institutions

CHAPTER 3:   The Log Cabin Quilt   71

CHAPTER 4:   The Immigrants   79

CHAPTER 5:   The Nation   89

PART III: The Quilts

CHAPTER 6:   The Cloth   111

CHAPTER 7:   The Tools   117

CHAPTER 8:   The Construction   119
      The Pieced Quilt/Borders/
      Backing and Batting/Quilting/
      Binding/Inscriptions

Epilogue   *155*

Notes   *158*

Bibliography   *161*

Index   *165*

ACKNOWLEDGMENTS

———————◆◆◆———————

A few of these small, soft links with another century have been
passed affectionately from one generation to another. Others have
found their way by often circuitous routes into distinguished
collections across the United States. The continuing generosity of
the individuals and institutions responsible now for their safe-
keeping has made possible my work in the research and exhibition
of this segment of America's past. I am grateful to them all:

America Hurrah Antiques; Larry and Myra Aronson; The
Baltimore Museum of Art, Dena S. Katzenberg, Consultant Curator
of Textiles; Darwin D. Bearley; Linda and Irwin Berman; The
Brooklyn Museum, Elizabeth Ann Coleman, Curator of Costumes
and Textiles; Edward Brown; Daughters of the American Revo-
lution Museum; Jeannette Fink; M. Finkel and Daughter; Ray and
Nancy Fisher; Frank and Lucy Flanigan; General Foods Corpo-
ration; Nancy Glazer; Evie Gleason; Robert Haas/Mariko Hibbett;
Phyllis Haders; Dr. and Mrs. Donald M. Herr; Jonathan Holstein
and Gail van der Hoof; Felicia Melero Holtzinger; Betty Horton;
Glendora Hutson; Janis Ito; Smith and Wanda Johnson; Kelter-
Malcé; George Kiberd and May Tow; Kiracofe and Kile; Phyllis
Kosloff; Marilyn and Ron Kowaleski; Dr. and Mrs. Roger Lerner;
Gloria List; Rosemarie and Richard Machmer; Marie Michal and
Peter Lubalin; Steve Miller American Folk Art; Bettie Mintz/'All
of Us Americans' Folk Art; Sandra Mitchell; Adrienne and Howard

ACKNOWLEDGMENTS

Moss; Museum of American Folk Art; The Natural History Museum of Los Angeles County; The Newark Museum, Ulysses G. Dietz, Curator of Decorative Arts; Parrish and Sons Antiques; Pilgrim/Roy; Private Collections; Linda Reuther and Julie Silber/ Mary Strickler's Quilt Collection; Freyda Rothstein; Stella Rubin; Carl and Elizabeth Safanda; Jackie and Stanley Schneider; Shelburne Museum; Smithsonian Institution, Doris M. Bowman, Division of Textiles; Society for the Preservation of New England Antiquities, Richard C. Nylander, Curator of Collections; Jim and Sandy Stephenson; B. J. Weldon; The Henry Francis du Pont Winterthur Museum; Yakima Valley Museum and Historical Society, Raymond E. Swenson, Curator of Collections; Ann M. Ziol.

The resources of the Textile and Costume Department of The Los Angeles County Museum of Art have consistently been made available to me through the generosity of its past and present curators, Mary Hunt Kahlenberg and Edward Maeder, and I am additionally grateful to Leslie Greene Bowman, Assistant Curator of Decorative Arts, for her reading of those portions of the manuscript pertinent to that area.

Josine Ianco-Starrels, Director of The Los Angeles Municipal Art Gallery, has made the facilities of that gallery available to me for two major exhibitions—the latter, in 1980, "Small Endearments: 19th-Century Quilts for Children and Dolls."

Janet Fireman, Curator of Cultural History at The Natural History Museum of Los Angeles County, was instrumental in my honorary appointment as a research associate with their history department, a position that has been invaluable to me in my study of the nineteenth century and the factors that shaped, and are reflected in, these small endearments.

Tom Vinetz was primary photographer for this publication and the results of his sensitive attention to its special requirements are evident on these pages.

Megan Schembre, my editor, has with faith and forbearance helped me to realize both in substance and style the book I had carried in my mind's eye. As with dozens of other projects, my husband's affection and assistance sustain the visions.

INTRODUCTION

◆◆◆

IN nineteenth-century America, the quilts that covered the
nation's sleeping children were an exquisite condensation of
the quiltmaker's craft. The quilts worked for children and
dolls were, simply and almost without exception, adult quilts
made small. The elements remained almost identical—the
size of the fabric pieces, the color and design are generally
unchanged—all were made "right" by a wonderful manip-
ulation of scale.

Unfortunately, the last decade has often tended to evaluate
nineteenth-century American quilts with singular attention
to those aesthetic considerations: dimension, color, and form.
It is an evaluation that too often unties the more subtle
threads that bound the quiltmaker to her work. In order to
fully understand these Small Endearments, we must recognize that beyond the elements of craftsmanship and design,
they reflect the cultural and social attitudes of a particular
place and time. They are the results of emotions, events,
and labors, filtered through the hands of women who were
writing, in thread, a journal of America and of childhood in
the nineteenth century.

These bits of calico and cotton focus on childhood as a

separate and distinct part of life, but it was a focus that did not exist four hundred years ago. The family unit itself did not emerge from previous feudal allegiances until the seventeenth century, and in the communal life of the Middle Ages, children were treated as the least of all creatures. The forces of European history began to shape the concept of "family." The power of the medieval priest and lord were transferred to the father, and this smaller unit was bound together by new and personal loyalties.

If the father was now assigned the position of absolute authority, the responsibilities of the mother in all levels of society were equally well defined: to attend to the household and to bear large numbers of children. This concept was translated intact from European events to the demands of a new nation, and a popular Colonial toast established those continuing priorities—"Our Land Free, Our Men Honest, Our Women Fruitful."

The rate of infant mortality was staggering. Only by continual childbearing could the eighteenth- and nineteenth-century woman fulfill her life's obligations: her obligation to God, as set down in the dictates of the Scriptures, that she should be fruitful and multiply; her obligation to her husband and family as each child represented an additional economic unit; and her obligation to her country, a pioneer society intent on expanding the population and the frontiers of a developing nation.

Women married young, bore children at regular and frequent intervals, and all too often died before middle age. Their deaths were, of course, ascribed to Divine Will. From the inscription of an eighteenth-century tombstone in Charleston, South Carolina:

Underneath
lies what was mortal of
Mrs. Margaret Edwards
Wife of Mr. John Edwards, Merchant of this place
Daughter of Mr. Alexander Peronneau, Gent
She Died
in Travail with her tenth Child
Aged 34 years and about 4 months
a Sincere, modest and humble Christian

. . . She committed her Soul to Him whom she ardently loved
and died without fear or a groan
Augt 27th, 1772.[1]

The dangers of childbearing and the great number of infant deaths must have created in most women a climate of unvoiced fears and resentments that precluded powerful sentimental attachments to their children. Newborns of the privileged class were most often given over to wet nurses and then to governesses or tutors. As soon as they were weaned, the infants of the poor became the responsibility of the older children. At the age of seven, according to his station in life, the child frequently left home to be educated or to be placed as an apprentice.

All this began to change, however, during the nineteenth century when the Industrial Revolution modified life-styles and better medical care enhanced the chances of survival for the young. Infant mortality was still high, of course, and throughout that century only an average of one out of five would live to see a fifth birthday.

Seven decades after Margaret Edwards "died in travail with her tenth child" another memorial 'marker' was worked of softer stuff. Nancy Ward Butler made this quilt to note

FIGURE 1. *Mourning quilt, 1842 (dated). Quiltmaker: Nancy Ward Butler. Jamestown, New York, 80" × 80". Cotton. Collection of the Smithsonian Institution.*

the death of her small granddaughter. It was worked full size—perhaps the extent of her sorrow could not be otherwise contained. In a life somewhat less harsh, women could allow themselves such emotional expressions of tenderness and affection for their children (Figure 1).

The nineteenth century was, in fact, a celebration of childhood, its opening chapters written in the eighteenth century by Locke and Rousseau. The nineteenth-century mother had been assigned a critical task—not just to bear large numbers of children, but to develop the innocence and individuality of those children for the greater glory of the Republic.

In her responsibility for the child, the mother was now ultimately responsible for the nation itself. The father remained the authoritative figure, but all aspects of the child's welfare depended on the wisdom with which his mother discharged her divine duty. In binding her family together with love as well as authority, she found herself guided every step of the way by the written word. By 1830, a vast number of treatises instructed her not only in the philosophical aspects of her duties but in specific and practical guidelines for every aspect of nursery life, from the child's health and dress to his education. If she was burdened by this new national responsibility, she was at least fortified by instruction from every possible source.

Just as society now required a woman to ensure her children's sleep, to make them safe and warm, the inclinations of her heart and hands now saw to it that they also slept in beauty. It is out of the sentimental attachments society now encouraged that these Small Endearments evolved—a fulfillment of society's dictates and sentiment's designs.

Images
and
Imagination

A NOTE ON DATING

The Small Endearments in this book represent one hundred years of American quilts and were worked from the beginning to the end of the nineteenth century.

In the dating information contained in the captions, the notation of a quarter-century (circa 1825) allows for maximum leeway. Decades (circa 1830) or half-decades (circa 1835) indicate a basis for a closer approximation. If a more exact date is entered (circa 1837), it is founded on some form of specific evidence. An actual date (1837) indicates the quilt has been documented or is dated and, if dated, that date has been determined to be the year of the quilt's construction rather than a commemorative notation or an addition.

All measurements are in inches, and width precedes length.

CHAPTER
ONE

REALITY

◆◆◆

BASKETS

THE Eastern Seaboard has always reflected its accessibility to
European goods and influences. As with their adult coun-
terparts, in both design and execution the earliest American
quilts for children and dolls were a reflection of European
tastes and fashions. But by the time the children of those
children had reached the Pacific Ocean, the history of the
American quilt had been written.

Almost all American women made quilts, and they taught
their daughters to make them. Soon a recognized vocabulary
of patterns and techniques had been developed and defined.
The quilts, like the country itself, were bound together by
threads of multiple and diverse origins. The images the
quiltmaker selected for reproduction were objects from her
surroundings, but the respondent chords they struck in the
observer drew on common experience.

In all cultures, the basket is a daily presence in a woman's
life. Light willow constructions, white oak egg baskets, schnitz
baskets to hold Pennsylvania's store of dried apples or
feathers—all were filled and emptied and refilled in the

eternal repetition of a housewife's duties. But baskets held not only the glories of her carefully tended orchards, but also the fruits of her creative labors—small bits of handwork and the small, simple tools with which they were worked. In whatever shape or material, it held the necessities of her life and the pleasures of her heart, and it somehow tied the American quiltmaker to long-dimmed traditions.

In its most elaborate form, a lattice basket was filled to overflowing with flowers, foliage, and fruit. As such, it became a common design throughout American decorative arts. It appeared early: carved by Samuel McIntire onto an elegant Salem mantelpiece, stitched by Suzannah Razor in 1783 on her delicate Dresden-work sampler, or cast in iron on a 1749 stove plate in Pennsylvania. It also flourished on the stenciled theorum paintings and watercolors done by the fashionable young ladies enrolled in the eastern seminaries. On nineteenth-century children's quilts that basket motif was worked in all the techniques of the craft—whole-cloth, *broderie perse*, all-white, appliqué, pressed, and pieced—in styles ranging from elegant to energetic.

Whole-Cloth

Through the advent of the new printing methods splendid fabrics were being manufactured abroad, and at the beginning of the nineteenth-century, American ports were waiting to receive this precious cargo. When home and self had been adorned, what better use for those last small bits of fabric, bought so dear, than to incorporate them into a child's quilt? These pieced fragments of a splendid pink-and-rose-colored Pillar Print (Figure 2) formed the backing for a small Flying Geese quilt. Variations of this type of design were popular both before and after the middle of the century—the pillars were topped with flowers—and here the lattice basket holds lush roses and leaves, plump grapes and tiny tendrils.

Broderie Perse

In the early part of the nineteenth-century, American women of the privileged class, whether of old money or new, seemed emotionally dependent upon European tastes. From the early importation of the Indian chintz that rose to such heights of fashion in England in the late seventeenth century,

FIGURE 2. *Flying Geese with Pillar Print backing (detail), circa 1840. Provenance unknown. 30½″ × 35″. Cotton. Collection of Marilyn and Ron Kowaleski.*

FIGURE 3. *Lattice Basket with floral border and stenciled frame, circa 1810. Provenance unknown. 40″ × 41″. Cotton. Collection of Linda and Irwin Berman.*

through the establishment of America's own beginnings in textile manufacture, the American housewife managed somehow to secure for herself in at least limited quantities the printed textiles most to her liking.

The expense of that early chintz import led her eventually to utilize even the smallest or worn sections of its bright patterns by carefully cutting out small elements from the printed motifs (flowers and buds, birds and leaves) and sewing them to a new background fabric in an arrangement designed to simulate the original whole-cloth. The technique, *broderie perse*, persisted in this country even after it had fallen into disuse in England and France.

The magnificent child's quilt worked in this exacting manner (Figure 3; also see Plates 2 and 3) reminds us that women used all of the refinements of the craft to enhance these children's quilts. Strips of fabric have been cut from several early pieces of cloth to form the lattice basket. When it was filled with flowers and leaves cut from other bits of chintz, additional clusters were arranged to form an inner border.

This quilt also boasts a stenciled inner frame, a technique not common on adult quilts and exceptionally rare on those done for children.

All-White

The color and design of the whole-cloth quilt were dependent upon the professional talents of others, and *broderie perse* allowed individual creativity primarily in the rearrangement of sections of that whole-cloth. The all-white quilt, however, was a comprehensive exercise in creative and technical excellence, and the result would be in many ways a measure of personal vanity. This quiltmaker would extract only the essence of the lattice basket, a line to be entered and embellished with simple needle and thread according to her individual talents.

This perfect piece (Figure 4. Also see Plate 5), worked in Marseilles quilting, is a remarkable refinement of both detail and workmanship. The basket is surrounded by delicate ribbons intertwined with the grapevines that support stuffed grapes and leaves. All this is contained within a three-inch oval band filled with the same oak leaves and acorns that adorned the Pillar Print (Figure 2). The outer fields are

FIGURE 4. *Lattice Basket (detail, all-white quilt), circa 1815. See* Plate 5. *Provenance unknown. 34" × 41" including 3" hand-knotted fringe. Cotton. Collection of Daughters of the American Revolution Museum.*

resplendent with vines, leaves, flowers, and grapes, all contained within a stuffed border. A handmade fringe completes this splendid effort.

In addition to infinite patience and a high level of skill, making this quilt would surely have required a special environment. It was most likely made for a child of the privileged class. A clean, quiet spot was seldom available to the quiltmaker in a small, crowded cabin. The fabric and fine thread were themselves unsuited to hands made rough by daily work.

Appliqué

The woman who worked the all-white quilt did not want color or pattern to distract the eye from the fineness of her stitch. For others, those "distractions" were desirable qualities. They were the paint, the clay, the silver, and the fibers from which others would construct their basket. Cutting a

FIGURE 5. *Lattice Basket (detail), circa 1850. See Plate 15. Provenance unknown. 44" × 44¼". Cotton and linen. Collection of Ann M. Ziol.*

shape from that colored cloth, the quiltmaker could work a bright basket of her own fancy. Here (Figure 5. Also see Plate 15) the basket is truly "constructed." It is interwoven from lengths of a striped cotton cut apart for the basket and for portions of the inner border. The basket was then filled with flowers of overlapping dimensions and further adorned with bits of embroidery, a grand gift for an anticipated grandchild.

Pressed

The pressed technique (fabric sewn onto a muslin base) was used principally for the Log Cabin design, or for a Crazy Quilt. It was not a technique that lent itself to the construction of an identifiable object such as a basket, but the random arrangements of silk and velvet on a Crazy Quilt often served as a background for an elaborately worked Victorian basket (Figure 6. Also see Plate 49).

FIGURE 6. *Lattice Basket (detail, Storybook Quilt), circa 1890. See Plate 49. Quiltmaker: Eudotia Sturgis Wilcox. Provenance unknown. 68″ × 78¼″. Predominantly silk and velvet. Western History Collection, Natural History Museum of Los Angeles County.*

FIGURE 7. *Baskets with Running Vine borders, circa 1895. Pennsylvania. 31" × 44". Cotton. Collection of Stella Rubin.*

Pieced

The extravagance of a whole-cloth quilt, an ambitious arrangement of *broderie perse*, the refinement of an all-white quilt, the elegant curved lines of appliqué, the basket almost obscured in the multiple images on a Crazy Quilt—these were most often considered to be the quiltmaker's best efforts. They were quilts that in technique and inspiration often reached back to European yesterdays.

But as with most European traditions, the quilt had been adapted to the needs of a new country through a simplification of shape and a clarification of line. In the pieced quilt (Figure 7), that intricate lattice basket has been reduced to its most simple elements, repeated in blocks across her quilt, a truly American quilt for an American child.

THE HEAVENS

Stars great and small shone brightly across this entire century of American quilts, and their multiple variations were translated intact from the beds of parents to the beds of children and dolls. For centuries the mysteries of the heavens had been passed from one generation to another: folklore and legend in the oral traditions of dimly remembered tales, ever-changing scientific theories in often crudely printed books and pamphlets, and, now, in quilted form. In these small doll quilts (Figure 8), needle and thread record the principal patterns through which women and their daughters interpreted the firmament.

FIGURE 8. Top left: *Lemoyne Star doll quilt, circa 1860. Lancaster County, Pennsylvania. 12" × 17½". Cotton. Collection of Evie Gleason.* Bottom left: *Starburst variation doll quilt, circa 1850. Provenance unknown. 11¾" × 12¼". Cotton. Collection of Linda Reuther, Julie Silber/Mary Strickler's Quilt Collection.* Top right: *Variabale Star doll quilt, circa 1845. Maine. 7" × 7¼". Cotton. Collection of Kiracofe and Kile.* Middle right: *Broken Star (single Dutch Rose block) doll quilt, circa 1855. Maine. 9¹/₁₂" × 10". Cotton. Collection of Kiracofe and Kile.* Bottom right: *Evening Star doll quilt, circa 1880. Berks County, Pennsylvania. 10¾" × 11". Cotton. Collection of Pilgrim/Roy.*

Although the pattern the quiltmaker called Variable Star (Figure 9) had been shaped by almost every culture that sought to work artistically within a square, the name she assigned to it seems particularly appropriate. The true astronomical characteristics of Variable Stars are that they ". . . vary in brightness, and frequently in other respects as well. These variations are fluctuations so that they do not permanently alter the configurations of the stars."[1] Through two centuries, the quiltmakers' choices of color and dimension and arrangement have at particular moments made the block extravagant or ordinary, brilliant or drab. As each quiltmaker approached the pattern, she returned to the same line to find another "fluctuation" in her own hands. Additionally, she found she could simulate the twinkling effect of the stars through variations in the outer line of her pattern and thus developed the Feathered Star (see Figure 14) and the Sawtooth Star (Figure 10).

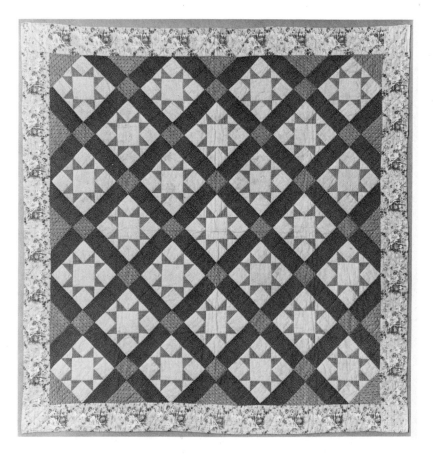

FIGURE 9. *Variable Star with whole-cloth glazed chintz border, circa 1850. Provenance unknown. 46″ × 47″. Cotton. Collection of Phyllis Haders.*

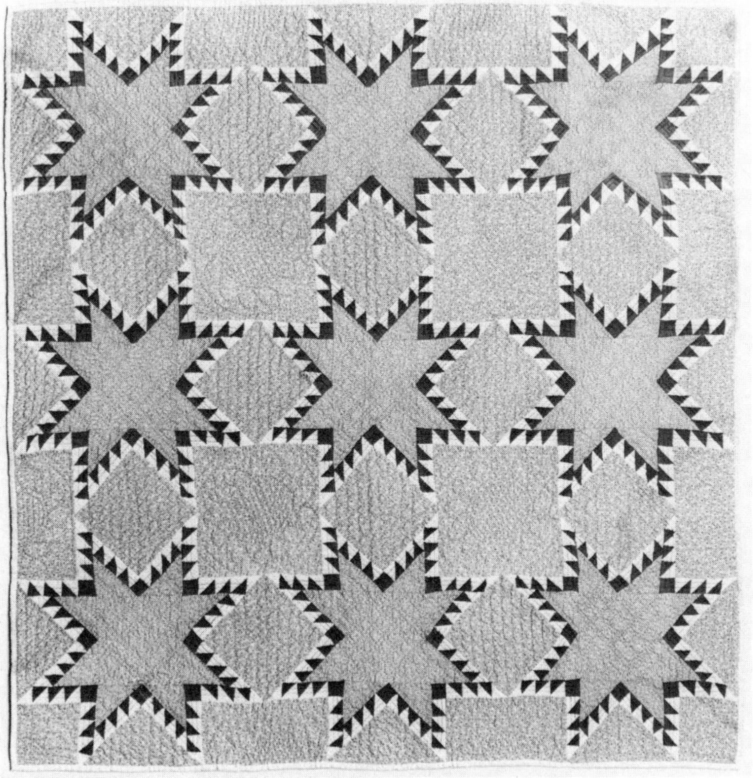

FIGURE 10. *Sawtooth Star, circa 1860. Maryland. 38¼" × 38¼". Cotton. Collection of Phyllis Haders.*

The size and splendor of the heavens were suggested in the massive motifs that radiated as single units from the center of full-size quilts. In the first quarter of the century, the Star of Bethlehem was worked in magnificent dimensions across quilts often nine feet square. Each star was composed of eight large diamonds, each of those diamonds itself composed of strips of smaller diamonds sometimes numbering in the thousands. The quiltmaker sought to arrange her glorious calicoes and chintzes in such a manner as to make the completed work appear to pulse and twinkle like the real thing. To an admiring quiltmaker of less talent and persistence, the sight of such a star spread across a bed would surely result in feelings of no less awe and reverence than she might have felt if she were looking upward into clear, dark skies.

The perfect construction of the Star of Bethlehem requires a high degree of technical excellence, and the fact that it was also worked on quilts for a child's small bed (Figure 11) attests to the fact that no pattern was considered too difficult to incorporate into those Small Endearments.

In an age intrigued by the idea that the heavens guided the destiny of man and nation, astrological images would also have been visible in some form to most nineteenth-century children. Standing on tiptoe a child might glimpse the intricate face of a John Fisher clock, ". . . as well as the signs of the zodiac and the seven planets of the pre-Copernican system; its astronomical dial has a moon face and stars and a planispheric map of the northern hemisphere with sunrises and sunsets indicated."[2] If a child were born in Lancaster, Berks, or York counties in Pennsylvania, perhaps his parents would have summoned the Mount Pleasant Artist to record the birth in *fraktur*-writing, including (as was his style) a painted clock indicating the time of birth. In almost every home there would surely have been an almanac,

FIGURE 11. *Star of Bethlehem with Sunbursts, circa 1875. Provenance unknown. 44" × 46". Cotton. Collection of Bettie Mintz, 'All of Us Americans' Folk Art.*

an astronomical and astrological guide to daily life in rural America filled with figures of lunar and solar eclipses, suggestions as to when to plant the crops, home medical remedies, and other bits of practical information. It was usually found hanging on a peg or nail available for easy reference.

Laura Russell (born in 1827 in Plymouth, Massachusetts) recalled her introductions to the diversities of astronomical theories. Her father believed long walks before breakfast led to a vigorous constitution and it was during those rambles they sometimes

> . . . fell in with an old sea captain who had a scientific turn of mind, and who among other pursuits, gave a great deal of time to astronomy. His ideas were somewhat peculiar; he believed our planet to be the center of the universe, and that the sun and moon and stars all revolved around it. The old man wrote a great many pages on this and other subjects and made numerous diagrams showing how the heavenly bodies were related to each other according to his ideas. At different times he lent my father these manuscripts to read, and we were much amused with the rude drawings and the extraordinary spelling which we found in them. One of them in particular contained a page covered with illustrations of the planetary system, the earth occupying a large space in the center, the orb of day being conspicuous for its absence. A small corner of the leaf was missing, and the old man had written in his crabbed characters around the ragged edge of the paper: "The sun's got tore out."[3]

The sky has always been a source of wonder, to illiterate and intellectual alike. The nineteenth century continued to be a time more of inquiry than of explanation but, as with the ancients, the observable regularities of the solar system were recognized and relied upon. They signaled the beginning and end of each day and marked the changing of the seasons, and as the North Star had guided so many across the great ocean so too would it eventually guide them across the continent.

Dependability was critical to the daily life of that still predominantly agrarian society. The quiltmaker celebrated the rising and setting of the sun with a number of patterns: Blazing Sun, Rising Sun, Harvest Sun. The Medallion quilt illustrated in Plate 32 would seem to cover the child with the comfort of that continuity, the Rising Sun dominating the center of the piece, separated by orderly compartments of stars.

FIGURE 12. *Crescent Moon, Diamonds, Hearts, and Sun doll quilt, circa 1860. New York. 17½" × 21½". Cotton. Private collection.* Courtesy of Nancy Glazer

That orderliness of things would not have been lost upon the child. Many diaries and recollections of nineteenth-century childhood recall the cycle of young lives in association with the changing of the seasons. Evelyn Ward recalled of her childhood at Bladensfield:

> We children had our jobs, any number of them. There was the sage to be picked for the sausage, the golden crab apples to be gathered for jelly, bags of chinquapins to be gotten in the warm sunshine behind the barn. . . .
>
> After frost came, chestnuts would be dropping freely. We would have to be out early every morning to pick them up before the hogs could get around to the trees and gather them for us. Often while out picking up nuts we would see the great red sun rising in the Autumn mist. . . .
>
> Our biggest job was to pick the cotton, but that would wait till November when the cotton balls would open. Father always raised a small supply of cotton that was picked by the children of the place, black and white. . . . Every summer we spent hours and hours paring fruit—peaches, quinces and apples—to be dried for winter use; now it was put in bags and spread along the windows on a sloping roof to catch the sun.[4]

But if the sky could seem familiar, it could also burst forth with frightening inconsistencies. A remarkable group of comets presented themselves throughout the nineteenth century, and among the most spectacular meteor showers of modern times were those that occurred in 1833 and 1866. At the peak of the 1833 display, the ten thousand meteors per hour that were visible over the eastern United States must have seemed to signify the end of the world to child and adult alike (Figure 13).

Sometimes, too, the seasons went awry (a frost too early, a drought too long) as did the seasons of young lives. As the younger children of Bladensfield were building warm memories of happy days in green orchards, the country was

FIGURE 13. *Starburst, circa 1855. Probably New England. 48" × 48". Cotton. Private collection.*

poised on the edge of a great Civil War, and before the seasons had once again gone full circle, Brother Will would be dead, and Brother Charlie, not yet eighteen, would be shot down in their beloved Virginia fields.

FLYING GEESE

Many natural occurrences were linked to the skies and to the seasons but few were as consistent and as visual as the migration of the great flocks of wild geese.

The direction those journeys took through the skyways had been set long ago. Just as a child and his parents might follow ruts worn deep in the Oregon Trail leading to the Pacific Ocean, so too did those other migrations follow routes already explored, airy paths that were remembered to offer food, water and—hopefully—at the end, safe haven.

The Ross's goose flew south across the plains, then turned west near Great Falls, Montana, to cross the Rocky Mountains. The blue geese traveled 1,700 miles from Canada's James Bay to coastal Louisiana. Others left their nesting grounds in Hudson Bay to feed in North Carolina from October until the first full moon in March.[5] Although the reasons behind those great movements were not understood, their reality was clearly noted on American quilts.

Shapes and forms familiar to the nineteenth-century quiltmaker were often distilled into abstract patterns and pieced into America's small quilts. The birds that flew in such profusion across those vast skies were seen through the needle's eye as simple triangles.

Small parts of those great flocks seem to tug impatiently at this lingering star (Figure 14), as if they are anxious for the night to be gone and their long journey begun again. In

FIGURE 14. *Feathered Star, circa 1840. New York State. 38" × 41". Cotton. Collection of Linda and Irwin Berman.*

Plate 12, the great star seems to have to compete for its place in a sky that will soon be filled with the circling Birds-in-the-Air and Flying Geese.

Flocks of geese were seen not only in the sky but in the fields where they fed or in the middle of a cold, dark pond where they felt most safe. And they were heard. The special sounds and signals they gave forth as they fed was soon replaced with shrill honking, an announcement the flock was about to resume the flight. That loud chorus could still be heard as they moved out in dark wedges across the sky. While father and son hunted the wild goose, mother and daughter were stitching for it a measure of immortality.

Rufus Porter, the remarkable itinerant limner who traveled on horseback and on foot throughout the New England and Atlantic states, left the artist's awareness of those magnificent flights on the walls of the Van Heusen farm in North Reading, Massachusetts (circa 1835–1840), and in Dr. Francis Howe's home in Westwood, Massachusetts, in 1838.[6] The simple dark V's on those frescoes became triangles of bright calico and chintz during those same decades.

The triangle, when joined into multiple units, offered the opportunity for a great diversity of pattern. Rows turned inward suggested the geese competing for food in the great stubbled fields, and these individual blocks could then be arranged in a variety of ways (Figures 15 and 16, Plate 22).

Every thrifty farm wife raised her own feathers, and she might choose to stitch the domestic goose (Plate 26), descended from the greylags, and sing about it to her drowsy children:

> *Go tell Aunt Rhody,*
> *Go tell Aunt Rhody,*
> *Go tell Aunt Rhody*
> *Her old gray goose is dead.*
> *The one she was saving,*
> *The one she was saving,*
> *The one she was saving*
> *To make a feather bed.*

FIGURE 15. *Wild Goose Chase, circa 1825. Provenance unknown. 32½″ × 42¼″. Cotton, including English printed textiles circa 1810–15. Collection of The Brooklyn Museum, Gift of Mrs. George Stonehill.*

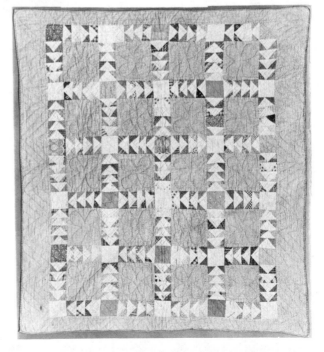

FIGURE 16. *Wild Goose Chase, circa 1860. Provenance unknown. 34″ × 37″. Cotton. Collection of the author.*

But most often the simple triangles were repeated in row after row of Flying Geese, long lines of simple shapes as a child might see them moving across a bright New England sky (Figure 17).

THE FORESTS

As they stood at last on the shores to which their long ocean voyage had brought them, America's earliest settlers saw a country of deep forests. In addition to shelter and fuel, those forests would yield symbolic imagery and creative inspiration. When the quiltmaker began to stitch small scraps of fabric into the American pieced quilt, she extracted elements from those piney woods to shape into variations of two patterns that would become classic and continuing. Small, sharp triangles forming pine trees seem to have been reserved for the pleasure of parents and are rarely found on nineteenth-century quilts for children. On these smaller pieces it was the softer lines of the oak leaf that were most often used.

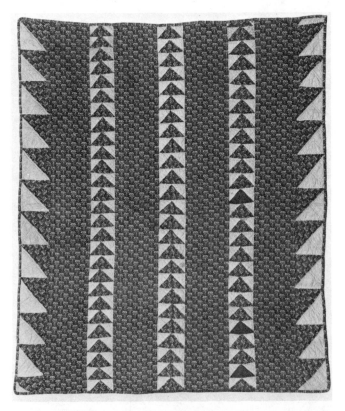

FIGURE 17. *Flying Geese with Sawtooth side borders, circa 1865. Pennsylvania. 35¾" × 41½". Cotton. Collection of Gloria List.*

The dense woods must have been a source of wonder, especially to those immigrants who had come from the treeless stretches of Holland and the Palatinate.

> I heartily wish for a dozen sturdy Tyrolese to fell the mighty oaks, for whichever way one turns it is *Itur in antiquam sylvam,* everything is forest.[7]

Such land was the scene of constant and urgent activity, for those giant oaks had to be brought down to clear the land for cultivation, the timber itself then used to shelter and warm a family.

Whether outside her cabin door or shaped into the uneven floorboards beneath her feet, the oak tree was incorporated into the life of quiltmaker and community. It was one of the woods used in the manufacture of the great Conestoga wagons as well as in the splint basket she held in her arms to carry her fruits and vegetables to market.

The oak tree was synonymous with strength and with the continuity of life. Although a deciduous tree, the oak clings stubbornly to its oldest leaves, refusing to drop them until the new growth replaces them in the spring. These were also personal characteristics necessary to each generation if the nation was to survive and expand. The symbol of those qualities was therefore both appropriate and meaningful when incorporated into a child's quilt.

The oak leaf was pleasing to the eye but, unlike the pine tree it was not adaptable to translation into the geometric shapes necessary for a pieced quilt. Appliqué provided the freedom of curved and flowing lines and allowed a more literal translation of this subject.

The shape of a single leaf was often used as an individual motif, perhaps to fill the open sections of an Irish Chain (Plate 44), worked into tiny quilted stitches, or used in border areas (Figure 18).

In the earliest and most classic arrangement, four oak leaves join at the center. In the most ambitious variations, the four leaves join with the elements of another early pattern, the Reel (alternate blocks, Figure 19).

FIGURE 18. *Center floral medallion with multiple borders, circa 1850. Probably New England. 40" × 41". Cotton. Collection of Linda and Irwin Berman.*

The two Oak Leaf and Reel patterns worked into children's quilts that are illustrated in this book attest to the inventiveness of the nineteenth-century quiltmaker in applying individual touches to the same traditional pattern. In Figure 20, the strength and texture of the oak tree itself have been ingeniously simulated through the choice of fabric—a sturdy, deep brown printed cotton. Worked in appliqué and reverse appliqué and very tightly quilted in a stipple pattern, this small quilt exudes a sense of sturdiness and purpose. In Saddlebrook, New Jersey, almost a half-century earlier, another quiltmaker had worked the same pattern into a quilt of less defined intent and focus (Plate 17). Delightfully unable to contain her enthusiasm for the myriad possibilities before her, she surrounded her Oak Leaf and Reel with a Trailing Vine border and, as if to confirm her mastery of all the quiltmaking techniques, she then completed her quilt with a wide border of pieced and appliquéd blocks of Carolina Lily.

FIGURE 19. *Oak Leaf and Reel with Sawtooth border, circa 1880. Pennsylvania. 32" × 42". Cotton. Private collection.* Courtesy of Steve Miller American Folk Art

This was always the challenge and the triumph of the nineteenth-century quiltmaker—to set down the classic patterns in a continuation of tradition and yet to make each piece, in its total presentation, as singular and new as if the pattern were hers and hers alone.

BOTANICAL OBSERVATIONS

Botanical study and observation was necessary for those early arrivals in the New World; the plants they would find or foster would be used for food, medicine, shelter, and clothing. Their survival and the development of the nation would depend on the identification and utilization of the country's natural resources.

In the middle of the eighteenth century, Karl Linnaeus, a Swedish botanist, produced a revolutionary reclassification of plants, and throughout the next one hundred years that study and the interest it generated had a profound influence on European decorative arts.

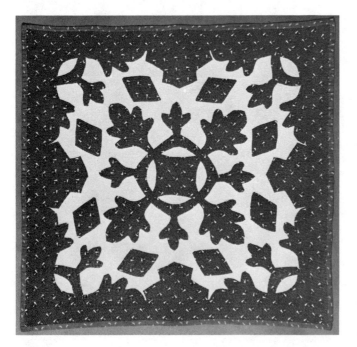

FIGURE 20. *Oak Leaf and Reel variation, circa 1895. New Jersey. 36" × 37½". Cotton. Collection of The Newark Museum.*

FIGURE 21. *Original design, circa 1860. Pennsylvania. 34" × 35¼".*
Cotton. Collection of Stella Rubin.

By the nineteenth century, studying botany in the United States had become fashionable as well as functional:

> Botany . . . is admirably adapted to the tastes, feelings, and capacities of females, as is demonstrated by the fact that the majority of botanists are females. Boys are less easily interested in it; more apt to be careless and harsh in their treatment of specimens, and too much attached to rude and boisterous sports. Girls, on the contrary, are apt to take delight in examining the most minute peculiarities of flowers, in pressing and preserving specimens, and in delineating the most remarkable with the lead pencil, or in water colours. Their enthusiasm, therefore, will generally be easily awakened.[8]

In addition to the pencil and the paintbrush, she had the needle and the thread, and what she found beyond her front door and in the open valleys and deep forests could be noted and preserved on America's quilts. Small quilts as well as large became botanical notebooks filled with leaves and vines, berries and buds.

Of all the flowers abloom on American beds, none seems to have been planted in greater abundance than the rose, and of all historic periods interested in the rose, none was more enthusiastic than the nineteenth century. Although the rose was preeminent in literature (Shakespeare referred to it on over sixty occasions) and was favored both as form and symbol by centuries of artists, early botanists seemed not to share those creative enthusiasms. Only fourteen types of roses appear in the revised edition of La Quintinie's *Herball* (1690) in contrast to the listing of more than four hundred varieties of tulips. Sixty years later Linnaeus speaks only of twenty varieties.

All this changed in the nineteenth century. Earlier horticulturalists did not suggest separate gardens for roses, and the first person to accord them concentrated boundaries seems to have been the Empress Josephine at Malmaison. With the introduction of a number of new roses, most especially the first hybrid tea varieties, rose gardens became

FIGURE 22. *Rose Wreath. Quiltmaker: S.D. (initialed). York County, Pennsylvania. 44" × 44½". Cotton. Collection of Phyllis Kosloff.* Courtesy of Nancy Glazer

FIGURE 23. *Whig Rose with Hearts and Swag border, circa 1875. Berks County, Pennsylvania. 40" × 41". Cotton. Collection of General Foods Corporation.* Courtesy of Bettie Mintz, 'All of Us Americans' Folk Art

fashionable. The flower became a favored embellishment on nineteenth-century costumes. The rose a quiltmaker wore on her hat or parasol also found a special spot on her child's quilt.

Reduced to its simplest shape (and usually cut from triple-folded cloth), the Foundation Rose was used singly or in wreaths (Figure 22, Plate 14) or as the basis for more complicated patterns. Arrangements of delicately shaded, overlapping appliquéd petals spilled from Baltimore Baskets. Bright bits of calico were shaped into a rose (Figure 23, Plate 37) that both Whigs and Democrats would call their own. Elegant silk and gaudy velvets were formed into dimensional bouquets on victorian Crazy Quilts (Plate 49).

One of the earliest and surely the most romantic rose pattern was the Rose of Sharon, drawn from the Song of Solomon. In the Biblical desert the "rose" was probably ". . . not a rose at all but an asphodel, while the Rose of Sharon is the name we give now to that most workaday of garden plants, St. John's Wort."[9] There were other botanical images, of course: the lily, the peony, currants and cock's comb (Figure 24), and berries in both blocks and borders.

The young girls so carefully sketching the flowers of familiar fields became the women who moved outward onto each new frontier that opened, and their letters and diaries are full of reminders of interests and pursuits now once again practiced out of necessity rather than the dictates of fashionable society:

> We have found the wild tulip, the primrose, the lupine, the ear-drop, the larkspur, and creeping holyhock, and a beautiful flower resembling the bloom of the beach tree, but in bunches as big as a small sugar-leaf, and of every variety of shade to red and green. I botanize and read some, but cook a "heap" more.[10]

FIGURE 24. *Currants and Cock's Comb, circa 1850. Provenance unknown.*
30½″ × 40½″. Cotton. Collection of Betty Horton.

FIGURE 25. *Rooster Crazy Quilt, circa 1880. New Jersey. 39" × 39½". Wool and cotton. Collection of Linda and Irwin Berman.*

FIGURE 26. *Horse and Dog Crazy Quilt, circa 1890. Pennsylvania. 39" × 47". Cotton and Velvet. Private collection.* Photo courtesy of America Hurrah Antiques

REFINEMENT

◆◆◆

ANIMALS

THE child of rural America has always shared its forests and fields with other creatures. Some were to be feared or hunted. Others were to be fed, sold, eaten—and these were often his responsibility within the family unit. This small Crazy Quilt (Figure 25) would seem to have been constructed for that farm child. The very fabrics used—substantial, serviceable cotton and wool—establish no pretensions, but are tenderly adorned with naive bits of embroidery depicting plants and farm animals. A glorious rooster struts across this multicolored barnyard. The sweep of his tail and the jaunty angle of his head suggest an attitude of confidence and importance, and in fact the outdoor life and physical labor he represented was a source of both individual and national pride.

The educational theories of Locke and Rousseau and increasing optimism regarding infant survival established new bonds of affection between the parent and the child, which in turn encouraged a new affection between children and animals. For the religious child, it was intended to extend beyond the benefits of simple companionship and amusement to instill in him a sense of responsibility and benevolence. Farm children had, of course, always had that responsibility, but now the appliquéd hearts surrounding the small dog and horse on this Pennsylvania quilt (Figure 26) seem reinforcement of simple and allowed affection.

The horse appears often on quilts for nineteenth-century children, but nowhere does it appear with more elegance than on the splendid all-white quilt worked by Meta Colt Toler of Newark, New Jersey, in the middle of the century (Figure 27). Graceful leaves done in stuffed work form a wide border inside the two-inch fringe that completes the piece. The quilt is an exercise in embroidered refinement,

FIGURE 27. *All-white quilt (detail), circa 1850. Quiltmaker: Meta Colt Toler, who has cross-stitched her initials in red thread on a back corner. Newark, New Jersey. 35½ " × 60" including a 2" fringe. Cotton and linen. Collection of The Newark Museum.*

red-on-white oval illustrations "A Representation of the Famous Match Race for 20,000. dollars aside between Mr. Van Ranst's horse Eclipse and Mr. Johnson's Horse Henry/ Run on the Long Island Course May 27, 1823."[3] The owners were Mr. Cornelius W. Van Ranst of New York and Col. William R. Johnson of Virginia, and in the third and final race Eclipse, a nine-year-old horse, won. The race was the first of thirty races run between the North and the South, and it drew over 50,000 spectators. Unable to match the intricate details of the copperplate print, the American quiltmaker could nevertheless piece her own tribute to another aspect of the sport, Steeplechase, (Figure 29). According to the prevailing theories of child raising, however, she may have done so at the peril of social criticism. The horse race was considered a dangerous source of temptation.

FIGURE 29. *Steeplechase, circa 1870. Ohio. 29" × 31¾". Cotton. Collection of Phyllis Haders.*

THE HORSE RACE

Who loves a horse race? Are not too many fond of it? Does it not lead to many evils, and to frequent ruin? Never go to a horse race. Mr. Mix had one child, whom he called Irene; he had also a good farm, and some money. He went to the races with his child, dressed in black crepe for the loss of her mother. Here Mr. Mix drank freely, and bet largely, and lost all he was worth. At night he went home a beggar; took a dose of brandy, and died before morning, leaving his child a penniless orphan. Never go to a horse race.

(from *The Clinton Primer*, 1830)[4]

Other horses pranced and leaped on the sides of America's barns and fences in the lithographed posters that signaled to American children the arrival of the grandest amusement of all, the circus! Although the clergy and many educators and newspapermen in a still strongly puritanical environment saw the circus as a true path to moral ruination, it continued to bring the wonders of the world even to backwoods America. The circus moved by whatever means of transportation was, at the time, joining the nation together—wagons along muddy roads, "floating palace" riverboats down the Mississippi and Ohio, and, at last, the railroad.

The elements of circus posters in a montage on the printed cloth form the center section of this tied comforter (Figure 30). The cameo shows an image of the classic Fool, the costume having originated in the commedia dell' arte, and the gladiator costume worn by the equestrian astride the two horses reminds us of the beginnings in ancient Rome. It has been noted that although the circus was born in Europe, it grew up in America.

In a country with our preoccupation with horses for pleasure, sport, farming, and transportation, the equestrian performances were of special interest. On a three-week tour in Hartford, Connecticut, Franconi's Colossal Hippodrome had advertised a "Grand Steeple Chase, Ladies and Gents on horses over hurdles and banners." On the fabric, a woman leaping over the banner is performing a variation on an act developed by James Robinson in 1856. Robinson was the

FIGURE 30. *Tied comforter. Whole-cloth center panel (circus print) with children's handkerchiefs, circa 1875. Probably Maine. 50" × 53". Cotton. Collection of Linda and Irwin Berman.*

best-known rider of that period; he turned somersaults over a banner under which his horse galloped. The scene of the handsome bareback rider and his clown assistant on the right, paper hoop held aloft, is remarkably similar to an 1870 poster. Horses are seen leaping through fiery rings with a daring rider. Normally horses will panic at fire, but Liberty horses were especially trained for this trick, although they generally performed alone.

The paper posters (STUPENDOUSLY MAGNIFICENT!, TEN THOUSAND WONDERS FROM EVERY LAND!, THE GREATEST SHOW ON EARTH!) eventually gave way to wind and rain and sun, but their images on this textile memory are still bright. To this lucky child, every day was circus day. He had truly "seen the elephant."

TOYS AND GAMES

Children's handkerchiefs, both imported and domestic, enjoyed great popularity throughout the nineteenth century. In 1810, using the first engraved rollers and machinery driven by water power, one man and two boys at the Bleach and Print Works of Thorp, Sidall and Co. near Philadelphia were able to print 10,000 yards of cloth or 50,000 children's handkerchiefs.[5]

Many such handkerchiefs spoke to the earlier and harsher views of a child's nature. One such piece (red on white cotton, illustrated, 15½ inches square) clearly set forth both content and purpose: "DISSECTED EMBLEMS suitable to the INSTRUCTION of YOUTH of all AGES. Designed to impress upon their minds a love to Virtue and Hatred to Vice." It reminded "the youth of EITHER SEX" that "JUSTICE WILL MOST ASSUREDLY OVERTAKE THE WICKED. MERCY FIRST AND LAST WILL BRIGHTEST SHINE."[6]

The later handkerchiefs present both in design and inscription a more enlightened approach to childhood, although they continue to ". . . speak of industry, temperance, patriotism and good children—subjects considered most important . . ."[7]

The handkerchiefs that surround the circus print in Figure 30 show us a splendid variety of those activities and interests judged suitable for the child's recreation and education, as indeed parents were encouraged to make those one and the same:

Top left: "Look at My Boat" reflects the same theme painted by Winslow Homer (*Ship Building*, 1873). Such play would prepare the child to practice the craft of the father, and on the Eastern Seaboard the business of the mariner was held in high esteem.

Center left: "Got a Bite." This enthusiastic angler might have been reprimanded by Catherine Beecher. Considered by many nineteenth-century mothers to be the authority on all things pertaining to family life, Miss Beecher believed that hunting and fishing for pure sport encouraged cruelty in children.

Bottom left: A similar scene of a boy and a girl blowing soap bubbles was printed on a handkerchief used in the quilt illustrated in Figure 31 (top left). Even an innocent pastime such as this could set a moral example. In *My Play Is Study*, published in 1855, the author suggests that meaningful lessons can be found in simple observations.

> The large bubble which burst so soon resembles the man who has risen and is thrown from his height, whilst the humble citizen continues his peaceful course like the smaller bubble unaffected."[8]

Top right: Like the children rowing in the handkerchief in Figure 31 (top right), these young people in the goat-drawn sleigh attest to the importance placed on outdoor activities. Increasingly, the value of fresh air and physical exercise was considered axiomatic.

Center right: One in a series of Chambers Miscellany of Useful and Entertaining Tracts called "The Management of Infants" suggested that ". . . prints of birds, or animals in general may be employed with great advantage, because they excite questions, afford the parent opportunities of giving much valuable oral instruction, and induce that love of enquiry, which is the parent of knowledge."[9]

Bottom right: "Shut your eyes and open your mouth/And see what the King will send you." This scene of two girls dangling a bunch of cherries before a young boy illustrates

FIGURE 31. *Handkerchief quilt with political bandannas, circa 1885. Provenance unknown. 40¼" × 52¾". Cotton and linen. Collection of Yakima Valley Museum and Historical Association.*

the type of game that was devised to utilize nature's own playthings and, in so doing, was considered particularly beneficial. Once the cherries had been consumed, the children could play yet another game, attempting to throw the cherry stones into a small hole in the ground.

The didactic qualities of checkerboard, cards, and dominoes (all included on the quilt in Plate 49) made them staples in the nineteenth-century toy cupboard, and the ideal family gathered in the evening to play a variety of games together. Toys that gave the child the opportunity to put things together and take them apart or knock them down and reassemble them encouraged not only dexterity but neatness, so time spent building houses of cards, or playing with dominoes or Tumbling Blocks (Figure 32) was time well spent. Play should always improve as well as amuse.

Games in the fresh air were of course encouraged. Blind

FIGURE 32. *Tumbling Blocks, circa 1860. Southington, Connecticut. 39¾" × 47". Cotton. Collection of the Smithsonian Institution.*

man's buff (illustrated on another handkerchief in Figure 31) was particularly helpful, according to Rousseau, in getting children used to the dark.

> When the shadows were long, and the evening breezes had cooled the earth, we little ones, whites and blacks, played Fox and Geese and Puss Wants a Corner . . . till we were called in for prayers and bed.[10]

Perhaps they went inside to sleep under a small quilt whose patterns had been inspired by those childhood games (Plate 27).

LITERARY INFLUENCES

The Bible was, of course, the principal literary presence in the American home. A number of pattern names were drawn from its pages but the only one widely used on a child's quilt seems to have been Jacob's Ladder. The influence of the Bible, however, was often noted by the quiltmaker's inclusion of a small and deliberate mistake, a religious error to attest to God's perfection in all things as opposed to the imperfection, however slight, of one's own work. This was generally accomplished with something as minor as an incorrectly turned triangle of fabric. Occasionally, however, as on this trundle quilt (Figure 33), extravagant piety will be displayed with the inclusion of a Humility Block, one that is technically of perfect construction but of an obviously differing fabric or pattern.

If there were one other, until well into the nineteenth century that book would in all probability have been John Bunyan's *Pilgrim's Progress*. This book was written in 1675 while the author was in prison for preaching the Gospel without official sanction and published three years later. Throughout the next two centuries it was printed and read more often than any book other than the Bible.

A masterful narrative, its popularity stemmed both from content and construction. It was written by a man who earned his living with his hands for those who did the same. For both author and reader, religion was an intimate part

FIGURE 33. *Union Star with humility block, circa 1865. Indiana. 55½″ × 67½″. Cotton. Collection of the author.*

of daily existence, and salvation was to be sought with the same spiritual earnestness displayed by Christian, Bunyan's young hero. It was written for common people, most of whom neither owned nor read many books, and it was therefore ideally suited to the majority of the populace of this new nation.

Pilgrim's Progress was read by children during this country's beginnings because, aside from the Bible, there were usually no other books to read. Except for occasional religious material, until the nineteenth century books were rarely written for children, and even then they were intended to instruct rather than to entertain.

By the beginning of the nineteenth century, however, the American child would have had access to *Robinson Crusoe*

(1719) and to *Gulliver's Travels* (1726). Both of these eighteenth-century English books were written for adults, but in addition to their political and social implications, they were splendid adventures. While Sir Walter Scott's popular epic poem *Lady of the Lake* (1810) might have introduced the child to the ancient traditions and tales of Scotland's loch country, it also provided his mother with inspiration for a quilt pattern whose design and name have remained unchanged for more than 150 years (Figure 34).

But either by choice—or because there was no choice—American children continued to read *Pilgrim's Progress*, and by the middle of the nineteenth century, their mothers had firmly established a classic quilt pattern inspired by a phrase that seems to have originated with that small book:

> . . . the Delectable Mountains . . . and behold at a great distance he saw a most pleasant, Mountainous Country, beautified with Woods, Vineyards, Fruits of all sorts, Flowers also, with Springs and Fountains, very delectable to behold. . . . And when thou comest there, from thence, said they, thou mayest see to the gate of the Celestial City. . . .[11]

When the Delectable Mountains pattern was worked on a small scale (Figures 35 and 36), it was worked for children to whom the pattern name was comfortably familiar.

Just as the Delectable Mountains continued to be worked into his quilt, we know from the children's literature of the last half of the century that the influence of *Pilgrim's Progress* was a continuing fact of the child's literary experience.

In 1858, Jacob Abbott published *Rollo on the Atlantic*, which began a series of books detailing the adventures of Rollo in Europe. It was the first series of books presenting the adventures of a child to achieve wide popularity in America, and "If there was any single symbolic hero of the age, it was little Rollo—only nine years old, yet the perfect hero of Abbott's ideals. Rollo was the spiritual heir of the Christian hero of *Pilgrim's Progress*. If this world was less terrible than Bunyan's and his earthly rewards more important, his character was just as disciplined and flawless. . . ."[12]

FIGURE 34. *Lady of the Lake, circa 1870. New York State. 41½" × 50½". Cotton. Collection of Phyllis Haders.*

While Rollo sought to avoid the corrupting influences of questionable companions and improper behavior, there was another popular character who seemed to seek them out. Huckleberry Finn, the quintessential American boy whose education came from the experiences of life itself, was touched by the book:

> This table had a cover made out of beautiful oil-cloth, with a red and blue spread-eagle painted on it, and a painted border all around. It come all the way from Philadelphia, they said. There was some books, too, piled up perfectly exact, on each corner of the table. One was a big family Bible full of pictures. One was *Pilgrim's Progress*, about a man that left his family, it didn't say why. I read considerable in it now and then. The statements was interesting but tough.[13]

In 1868 Louisa May Alcott published *Little Women*, and the influence of Bunyan's book is both obvious and pervasive. Chapter titles draw on Bunyan's phrases ("Beth Finds *The*

FIGURE 35. *Delectable Mountains variation, circa 1860. Pennsylvania. 41½" × 43". Cotton. Collection of George Kiberd and May Tow.*

Palace Beautiful," "Meg Goes to *Vanity Fair,"* and *"The Valley of the Shadow,"* for example) as does conversation throughout the book. ("We were in the Slough of Despond tonight, and Mother came and pulled us out as Help did in the book. We ought to have our Roll of Direction, like Christian."[14])

Little Women is more than the story of Jo and her sisters— it follows the progress of four pilgrims. In the first chapter, "Playing Pilgrims," Mrs. March (Marmee) asks:

> Do you remember how you used to play Pilgrim's Progress when you were little things? Nothing delighted you more than to have me tie my piece-bags on your backs for burdens, give you hats and sticks and rolls of paper, and let you travel through the house from the cellar, which was the City of Destruction, up, up to the house-top, where you had all the lovely things you could collect to make a Celestial City.[15]

and Beth responds:

> My favorite part was when we came out on the
> flat roof where our flowers and arbors and pretty
> things were, and all stood and sung for joy up
> there in the sunshine. . . .[16]

Almost two hundred years had passed since the first pilgrim
had caught sight of the Delectable Mountains.

From a piece-bag such as Mrs. March had tied to Jo's back,
the American quiltmaker could select bits of fabric to build

FIGURE 36. *Delectable Mountains with Double Zigzag border,
circa 1870. New Jersey. 37″ ×
56″. Cotton. Collection of Linda
and Irwin Berman.*

for herself a Delectable Mountain that would cover and comfort her own small pilgrim.

The silk and velvet extravagance worked by Eudotia Sturgis Wilcox as a Storybook Quilt for her granddaughter (Plate 49) indicates by fabric and design the changes that a century had brought to the American quilt. By the same token, its subject matter illustrates the great changes that had occurred during the last quarter of the century in children's literature. The earlier literary concentration on the development of the child's character now yielded to the development of the child's imagination. Stories of adventure and fantasy were both accepted and encouraged. The literature, like this quilt, was truly meant to delight.

In addition to the traditional scattered motifs (fans, butterflies, horseshoes, etc.), the illustrations stitched in realistic details record the elements of fantasy and fable that had been introduced into this golden period of children's literature. The detail of Heidi and her Grandfather (Figure 37) introduces European adventures to the American child, but this quilt is predominantly a collage of America's history as seen in its children's books.

American literature of the last quarter of the nineteenth century was often preoccupied with local character, mannerisms, and speech. Such American regionalism is noted on Wilcox's quilt in the detail of Uncle Remus—his face, like the others, is carefully and realistically painted on soft glove leather (Figure 38). The book from which this character was drawn—Joel Chandler Harris's *Uncle Remus, His Songs and His Sayings: The Folk-Lore of the Old Plantation* (1881)—was immensely popular in the decade during which this quilt was made.

In Brunswick, Maine, a thirty-nine-year-old mother of six had earlier written another part of this domestic southern history. Moved by The Fugitive Slave Act and inspired by "a vision," Harriet Beecher Stowe sat down to write what would become the concluding chapter of a melodramatic novel that would help to alter the course of the nation. *Uncle Tom's Cabin*, published in serialized form in 1851, met with the same widespread popularity that had been accorded *Pilgrim's Progress*. The two were dissimilar in style (Mrs. Stowe wrote not in simple, direct language but with a sentimentality

FIGURE 37. *Detail of Storybook Quilt, circa 1890.* Left: *Uncle Tom and Little Eva.* Right: *Heidi and Grandfather. See Plate 49. Quiltmaker: Eudotia Sturgis Wilcox. Provenance unknown. 68″ × 78¼″. Predominantly silk and velvet. Western History Collection, Natural History Museum of Los Angeles County.*

similar to that of the Brontës), but both spoke with great earnestness and conviction to the common conscience. In spite of the book's literary weaknesses, the emotional aspects of her subject were so clearly focused that sides were drawn and defined on the issues she addressed.

Although *Uncle Tom's Cabin* was written for the adult, its message was wrapped in adventures grand enough to satisfy the child. Mrs. Stowe also condensed its content for the

FIGURE 38. *Uncle Remus (detail, Storybook Quilt), circa 1890. See Plate 49. Quiltmaker: Eudotia Sturgis Wilcox. Provenance unknown. 68" × 78¼". Predominantly silk and velvet. Western History Collection, Natural History Museum of Los Angeles County.*

youngest among them, for this was an age that strongly felt the nation to be only as good as its children. *Pictures and Stories from Uncle Tom's Cabin* was published in 1853. To emphasize the moral importance of the sentimental illustrations, the preface to the small book reads:

This Little Work
Is Designed To Adapt
Mrs. Stowe's Touching Narrative
To The Understandings Of The Youngest Readers
And To Foster In Their Hearts
A Generous Sympathy For The
Wronged Negro Race of America[17]

When Eudotia Wilcox worked her quilt, the Civil War had been fought and the issue decided. Her images are a kindly old black man and a sweet blond child, Uncle Tom and Little Eva, in bits of silk and velvet and sentimental recollection (Figure 37).

The geometric symmetry of the sturdy Delectable Mountains was intended to suggest to the child the spiritual rewards of piety and obedience. The Storybook Quilt illustrates the material rewards of American industry and ingenuity—with its center figure a young girl in silk and lace, a parasol on her shoulder, and a flower in her bonnet.

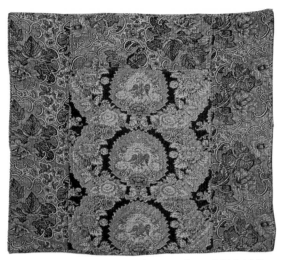

PLATE 1. *Whole-cloth quilt, "Eagle and Shield from Seal of the United States," circa 1825. Provenance unknown. 42¼" × 37". Cotton. Collection of The Baltimore Museum of Art, gift of Dena S. Katzenberg.*

PLATE 2. Broderie perse *quilt. Chintz appliqué of floral and bird motifs with Dog's Tooth border, circa 1825. Provenance unknown. 30" × 34". Cotton. Collection of Linda and Irwin Berman.* Photograph courtesy of America Hurrah Antiques

PLATE 3. Broderie perse *quilt. Chintz appliqué of floral and bird motifs with inner whole-cloth border, circa 1825. Provenance unknown. 64" × 68". Cotton. Private collection.* Courtesy of Kiracofe and Kile

PLATE 4. *All-white quilt with stuffed work, circa 1825. New England. 40" × 39", including a 6" fringe border on three sides. Cotton. Private collection.* Photograph courtesy of America Hurrah Antiques

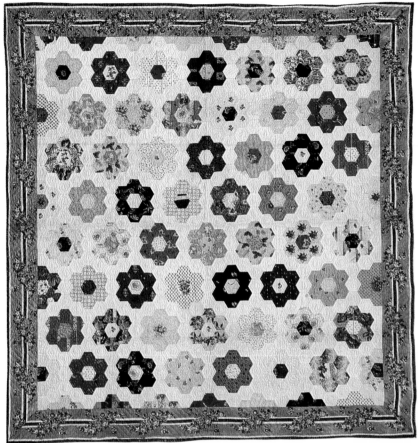

PLATE 8. *Hexagons with whole-cloth border, circa 1825. Provenance unknown. 48¼" × 50½". Cotton. Collection of Larry and Myra Aronson.* Courtesy of Edward Brown

PLATE 9. *Hexagons with whole-cloth border, circa 1825. Provenance unknown. 40¼" × 45¾". Cotton. Collection of Bettie Mintz, 'All of Us Americans' Folk Art.*

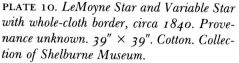

PLATE 10. *LeMoyne Star and Variable Star with whole-cloth border, circa 1840. Provenance unknown. 39" × 39". Cotton. Collection of Shelburne Museum.*

PLATE 11. *Variable Star with inner Sawtooth border, outer whole-cloth border, circa 1835. Provenance unknown. 34½" × 39¾". Cotton. Collection of Edward Brown.*

PLATE 12. *Star of Bethlehem with multiple borders, circa 1825. Sometime during the next quarter-century, a small circle was appliquéd to the center of the star. It bears a partially illegible inscription: "When Ever the . . . Dearest . . . Think of Me. From Mary to Eliza." Provenance unknown. 46" × 46". Cotton. Collection of Jeannette Fink.*

PLATE 13. *Sawtooth Star medallion with Sawtooth, Ninepatch, and whole-cloth borders, circa 1840. Pennsylvania. 40" × 42". Cotton. Collection of Stella Rubin.*

PLATE 14. *Rose Wreaths with multiple Flying Geese borders, circa 1850. Kees Homestead, New York. 51½" × 59½" Cotton. Collection of Dr. and Mrs. Roger Lerner.*

PLATE 15. *Lattice Basket with Swag and floral borders, circa 1850. The partially illegible inscription beneath the basket of interwoven fabric reads: "Presented to Mrs. Margaret M. C . . . by her Mother." See Figure 5. Provenance unknown. 44" × 41¼". Cotton and linen. Collection of Ann M. Ziol.*

PLATE 16. Top left: *LeMoyne Star and Bachelor's Puzzle doll quilt, circa 1865. New England. 9¼" × 9¼". Cotton. Collection of Marilyn and Ron Kowaleski.* Top right: *Bachelor's Puzzle doll quilt, circa 1875. Lancaster County, Pennsylvania. 9" × 9½". Cotton. Collection of Bettie Minz, "All of Us Americans" Folk Art.* Middle: *Nine-patch doll cradle quilt, circa 1860. Pennsylvania. 5¾" × 14". Cotton. Private collection. Courtesy of Evie Gleason.* Bottom: *Two-patch medallion with Sawtooth border doll quilt, circa 1850. New England. 15½" × 15½". Cotton. Collection of Glendora Hutson.*

PLATE 17. *Oak Leaf and Reel variation with Trailing Vine inner border and Carolina Lily outer border, circa 1850. Saddlebrook, New Jersey. 40" × 40". Cotton. Collection of Jeannette Fink.*

PLATE 18. *Hexagons, circa 1850. A narrow soutache forms the Running Vine border and incorporates tiny stuffed berries and buds, with a peony in each corner. Provenance unknown. 32" × 33". Cotton. Collection of Phyllis Haders.*

PLATE 19. *Peony variation center block with outer border of divided Rising Sun signature blocks, circa 1875. Provenance unknown. 25³/₄" × 26¹/₄". Cotton. Collection of Nancy Glazer.* Courtesy of Evie Gleason

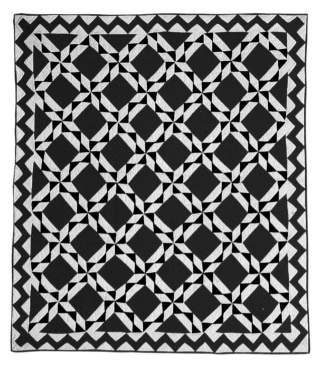

PLATE 20. *Ocean Waves variation, circa 1880. Provenance unknown. 42¹/₂" × 47¹/₄". Cotton. Collection of Stella Rubin.*

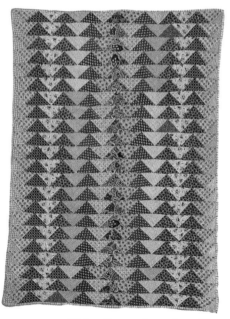

PLATE 21. *Flying Geese, circa 1830. New England. 27" × 38". Cotton. Collection of Frank and Lucy Flanigan.* Courtesy of Edward Brown

PLATE 22. *Wild Goose Chase, 1880 (dated). See Figure 108. Maryland. 39³/₄" × 37¹/₂". Cotton. Collection of Adrienne and Howard Moss.* Courtesy of Stella Rubin

PLATE 23. *Walk Around*

PLATE 24. *Variable Star and Nine-patch*

Reversible quilt made to commemorate the birth of Alfred P. Sawyer on August 20, 1856. See Figure 94. Lowell, Massachusetts. 50" × 50". Cotton. Collection of George Kiberd and May Tow.

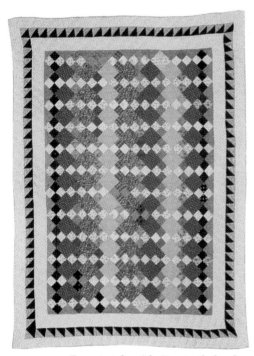

PLATE 25. *Four-patch with Sawtooth border, circa 1870. Dayton, Ohio. 31¼" × 43". Cotton. Collection of Freyda Rothstein.*

PLATE 26. *Brown Goose/Gray Goose with Flying Geese border, circa 1875. Provenance unknown. 30" × 36". Cotton. Collection of the author.*

A REFLECTION OF
THE DECORATIVE ARTS

The pineapple, America's traditional symbol for hospitality, was worked by Rachel Smith into an all-white child's quilt of formal arrangement and classical influence (Figure 39). The same motif, with a more subtle quilted line replacing the dimensional effect Rachel achieved through her careful stuffed work, appears in all four corners of the small quilt illustrated in Plate 37. If the quiltmaker fancied a pineapple of colored and printed cloth, the true shape of the object could still be worked in a pictorial manner (Figure 40). If the shape could be drawn, it could be worked in appliqué.

Unless she chose to cut freehand or from pieces of folded fabric (as for Foundation Roses or some random leaves), the quiltmaker marked the true shape and size of the desired element on the reverse of the cloth. She cut one-quarter

FIGURE 39. *Pineapple (detail, all-white quilt), circa 1870. Quiltmaker: Miss Rachel Smith of Derby, Connecticut, designed and worked this quilt while visiting her grandniece, Mrs. John B. Morris. Newark, New Jersey. 38½" × 59" including a 2" fringe. Cotton. Collection of The Newark Museum.*

FIGURE 40. *Pineapple doll quilt, circa 1875. Pennsylvania. 21¼" × 19½". Cotton. Collection of Jonathan Holstein and Gail van der Hoof. In the center of the quilt, the name "Sallie J. Davault" is surrounded by finely sketched leafy boughs.*

FIGURE 41. *Princess Feather, circa 1890. New York State. 36½" × 37". Cotton. Collection of Felicia Melero Holtzinger.*

inch beyond that line, clipped the curves where necessary, and (to retain the accuracy of the shape required) turned under and basted that seam allowance. The design, or its multiple components, was then arranged on the ground cloth and broadly basted into place. Occasionally the edges would be secured with a decorative stitch (buttonhole, overcast, or running), but the exceptional needlewoman, or she who aspired to that designation, would work the finest stitch

FIGURE 42. Broderie perse *quilt with whole-cloth border, circa 1840. Quiltmaker: H. V. (cross-stitched initials on a back corner). Provenance unknown. 41½″ × 55¼″. Cotton. Collection of Bettie Mintz, 'All of Us Americans' Folk Art.*

she could manage, a blind stitch, invisible to the eye. Soft curves were relatively easy; the true test of her skill was demonstrated in the selection of a pattern such as Princess Feather (Figure 41) with its multiple angles and indentations.

Those pineapples worked on the doll's quilt either by or for Sallie Davault were drawn from a vocabulary of designs common to American craftsmen working in all media. The decorative arts of the eighteenth and nineteenth centuries had a profound effect on the American appliqué quilt in terms of the selection and arrangement of motifs.

The motif was often drawn from the fabric itself. The early preferences for imported chintz as an adornment for bed and bed hangings could be realized only by those of substantial means. They were simulated, however, at a cost far less dear through the technique of *broderie perse*. Rather than buying large pieces of the chintz, the quiltmaker could cut motifs from a smaller piece, or from the remnants of another cutting, to rearrange and appliqué to a plain ground (Figure 42).

Napoleon's preferences in furniture and fashions were echoed in this country in wood, silver, glass, and cloth. A third "Crown of Charlemagne" had been created for his coronation, but he chose instead to crown himself emperor with a golden wreath of laurel leaves, the traditional symbol for victory that he had chosen as his personal emblem. Those leaves were translated into humbler stuff for American quilts—in this case, they were crossed sprays of red and green for some Massachusetts child (Figure 43).

French and English wallpaper were among the early imports to the colonies, and by 1739 Plunkett Fleeson was selling paper of his own manufacture in his Philadelphia shop. The expensive rolls, like the large pieces of chintz, were beyond the financial means of most households and beyond the physical reach of rural areas. The itinerant craftsman, however, offered an acceptable alternative through the use of his paint, brush, and stencil patterns. Although the decorative patterns he worked on those early walls followed many of the arrangements found on wallpaper, the intricacies of the paper designs were difficult to reproduce in the time allotted to him by a housewife's limited budget.

FIGURE 43. *Laurel Leaves, 1850. Quiltmaker: Mrs. L. G. Richardson. Woburn, Massachusetts. 40" × 40". Cotton. Collection of Glendora Hutson.*

As with almost every fashion or European import, the designs were simplified and adapted to American preference and practicality. The stenciled motifs generally accommodated larger areas of white space in separating the sections of design and borders.

The bold patterns employed pigments usually made from materials at hand (clay, brick dust, lampblack). Dry colors were available for purchase, however, and most often were mixed with skimmed milk. The colors were applied to the white plastered walls, and in the nineteenth century, many of the designs found on those earlier walls were worked with equal intensity and enthusiasm onto the white ground of a child's quilt.

This was particularly true in the use of the swag border. Embellished with bell or with tassel, it was a design also used in plasterwork ornamentation and on furniture. For the quiltmaker, paper, paint, plaster, and wood were replaced by cotton, often in combinations of turkey red and Victoria green, to enclose the interior elements of design on quilts both large and small (see Plates 38 and 43).

The American housewife who could afford the chintz and the wallpaper could in all probability afford to set her table with imported porcelain. Here, too, another acceptable alternative became available to the increasingly large middle class. In the early decades of the nineteenth century, blue and white pottery, transfer printed, arrived in America in large numbers and of moderate cost. The borders of these platters and plates (many of Staffordshire origin) are rich with flowers and the oak leaves and acorns that encircle American quilts.

In the middle of the nineteenth century, in Baltimore and its surrounding area, the art of appliqué had come to full and formal flower on a remarkable group of quilts that have come to be collectively known as Baltimore Album Quilts. It is a unique body of work characterized by remarkable consistencies in design and execution.

A special quilt of particular interest is a Baltimore Album child's quilt (Figure 44; also see Plate 7), the small fruit of those larger cultural and creative labors. The provenance of the piece strongly indicates that it covered a Pennsylvania child, but its similarities to the Maryland quilts are unmistakable and could be explained in a number of ways. It may well have been worked as the result of a visit to, or a visitor from, that sophisticated city. The turnpikes between Baltimore and Pennsylvania that carried the goods of commerce could also have carried this small quilt or perhaps its thoughtful beginings.

The motifs worked in the appliquéd blocks are the same, although simplified. Similar épergnes, lattice baskets, and cornucopias are filled with flowers in stylized compositions. The quiltmaker worked multifloral branches in both open and closed wreaths of neoclassical ornamentation and in sprays both crossed and tied. The motifs were, of course, not unique to the Baltimore quiltmaker: the lyre she used was also found on Duncan Phyfe's New York chairs, on the foot pedal support of a Boston concert grand piano by Jonas Chickering, on a castiron parlor stove, and below a bust of Jenny Lind on a bottle of aquamarine blue.

The work is finely stitched, although with less elaboration and distinction. Two elements of construction consistent with

FIGURE 44. *Baltimore Album Quilt (detail), circa 1845. See Plate 7. Pennsylvania. 44¾" × 58½" including 3" fringe. Cotton. Private collection.*

several Baltimore quilts appear on this smaller work: sections of reverse appliqué used in identical tulips, and several flowers and basket handles formed of overlapping "coins" of fabric.

The rainbow, or "fondu," prints, used so effectively by the Baltimore ladies (single-color fabrics with a gradual intensity of shading) are not present on this child's quilt. The border print, however, strengthens the creative connection. If one looks closely at the segments that cling stubbornly to the cotton batting, one can still discern the colors (gold, red, and black) and the faint shapes of the acanthus scrolls and leaves that were used in the French Restoration-style fabrics. This fabric is similar, if not identical, to the border fabric and to certain elements of appliqué used in at least three full-size Baltimore Album Quilts.

Sashing and border have been almost lost to time and deterioration, the fringe is now tangled and irregular, but love and a sense of continuity have protected this special treasure as it passed from one generation to another, unbroken threads tying together a century and a half of family.

The Industrial Revolution made available to women even in fixed economic circumstances an increasing number of possessions, and the adornment of every square inch of the Victorian Crazy Quilt is in keeping with the trends of the period in the decoration of its parlors. The silks and satins, the beading and brocades, the laces and ribbons and velvets are hardly the stuff of which one would expect a child's quilt to be worked. No matter how elegant the fabric or the technique, the elements in most children's quilts allowed for the occasional need of soap and water. The majority of the small pieces identified by contemporary observers as Crazy Quilts for children were in fact intended to cover a piece of furniture rather than a small child. Most were worked to spread over a table, or put on a piano, or drape on a sofa— to decorate the interior of one's home rather than to comfort the delight of one's heart. It is unreasonable, however, to think that *none* of the American quiltmakers made one of these sentimental statements to cover her most precious possession.

When these extravagances were worked for children, they most often assumed the dimensions of a lap robe. As with the Storybook Crazy Quilt (Plate 49), they were intended more to entertain than to envelop. Occasionally on the smaller pieces, however, one interprets a particular set of motifs or written words, or simply feels intuitively that the piece was truly meant to cover a child, if only briefly. A small bit of Victorian whimsy was surrounded with the additional impracticality of a wide lace flounce—but in the center of the quilt its purpose has been made clear by the embroidering of "Baby Gay" (see detail, Figure 45). Bottles are also prominently featured, and if the centered forms can be interpreted to be hops, is it possible that Baby Gay was the special pride of a brewer's wife?

FIGURE 45. *Crazy Quilt (detail), circa 1890. Provenance unknown. 36″ × 31½″. Predominantly silk with a 3″ cotton lace ruffle. Private collection.*

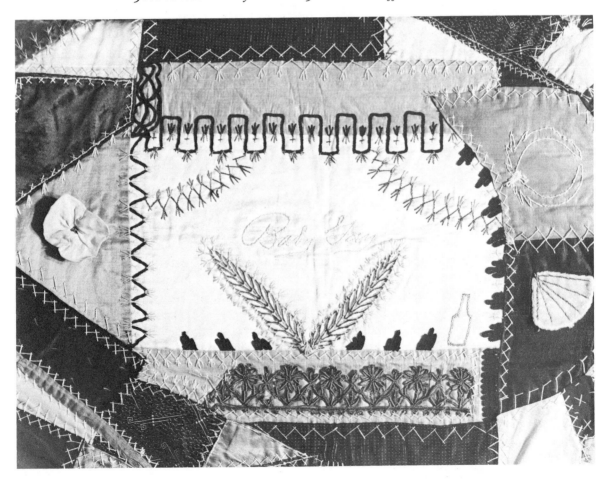

FIGURE 46. *Contained Crazy Quilt, circa 1835. Pennsylvania. 39" × 39". Cotton. Private collection.* Photograph courtesy of America Hurrah Antiques.

The beginnings of the Crazy Quilt, however, are written in cotton and wool, often scraps and remnants on the edge of deterioration. Individual and random pieces of fabric were sewn directly onto pieces of muslin, or even onto additionally fragile squares of remnants. In this pressed technique, the whole became stronger that the parts. On occasion, even when worked in these humbler fabrics, the choice of pattern was dictated by fashion, and the segments of crazy patches are set into final form with extraordinary formality (Figure 46). Because the constructed unit was most often a square or rectangle, there is inevitably a natural source of order, even when the material is of undistinguished origin (Figure 47).

FIGURE 47. *Crazy Quilt, circa 1870. Pennsylvania. 43" × 49". Cotton. Collection of Linda and Irwin Berman.* Photograph courtesy of America Hurrah Antiques

The random arrangement of a Crazy Quilt by the use of the same technique can give way to the more rigid linear organization of the American Log Cabin quilt. In this transitional piece (Figure 48), it is as though the diverse elements of America are surrounded by a more clearly defined intent—the crossing of America's frontiers. The Log Cabin quilt became its symbol.

FIGURE 48. *Crazy Quilt with Log Cabin border, circa 1885. Pennsylvania. 40" × 61". Cotton. Collection of Linda and Irwin Berman.*

*Individuals
and
Institutions*

CHAPTER
THREE

THE LOG CABIN
QUILT

◆◆◆

In the quilts that covered Amish children, we see a tradition turned inward, a reinforcement of borders and limitations, the encouragement of boundaries. In the Log Cabin quilts, we see the symbol of American arms thrown open to embrace the whole continent.

Even before the Revolutionary War, individuals and their families began to detach themselves from the Eastern Seaboard. Their first travels were along little more than pathways in the forests. The great river systems determined the earliest routes of internal migration until the French and Indian Wars opened the way for more secure expansion over land routes. Even then, the Western "roads" were only wide enough for a horse or small cart. In the first decade of the nineteenth century, there was not a wagon road west of the Appalachias, and not until the roads were widened and improved did we see the great canvas-covered wagons we associate with the opening of the frontier. There was, in fact, a succession of frontiers—forests and mountains and prairies and deserts each being conquered until at last the Pacific Ocean was in sight.

In 1838, an English observer standing at the edge of the forest along the Mississippi River noted:

> A few miles farther on, we went ashore at the wooding-place, and I had my first walk in the trodden forest. The height of the trees seemed incredible, as we stood at their foot, and looked up. It made us feel suddenly dwarfed. We stood in a crowd of locust and cotton-wood trees, elm, maple, and live oak: and they were all bound together by an inextricable tangle of creepers, which seemed to forbid our penetrating many paces into the forest beyond where the wood cutters had intruded.[1]

It was into that vast "wooding-place" that American children walked, and across the dry prairies and high mountains that they rode and struggled. It was a journey fraught with peril for those young spirits:

> We had an empty cracker box which we made answer for a coffin, dug a grave in the middle of the road and deposited the dead child therein. ... We filled the grave with stones and dirt, and when we rolled out, drove over it. Perhaps we had cheated the wolf by so doing—perhaps not.[2]

But for the child who survived, there was a splendid tale to tell, for he was a part of America's great adventure.

In 1845, an editorial in the New York *Morning News* added a new phrase to the American vocabulary. It was declared to be our "Manifest Destiny" to "overspread and to possess the whole of the continent for the great experiment of liberty," and western expansion became a patriotic preoccupation. Even the child who remained in Virginia or Maine was caught up, in the middle of the century, by a nation moving West. He was entranced both by the myths and by the realities.

The western movement began slowly, but with the rapid acquisition of land, the major boundaries began to fall— Texas in 1845, Oregon in 1846, California in 1848, and additional portions of the Southwest following the Gadsden Purchase in 1853. Although the American frontier was not historically to close until 1890, America's great dream was realized. The symbol for that dream, and for the individual qualities that made it a reality, was the log cabin, a simple structure that was one of the most important elements in the rapid expansion to the Pacific Ocean.

To enter those first forested frontiers, a father had to be assured that within that hostile environment he could provide, at the end of the journey, immediate shelter for the family that walked beside him. The answer to that principal concern was a modification of a structure brought with the Swedish settlers when they left their similarly wooded homeland to establish New Sweden in the Delaware Valley in 1638.

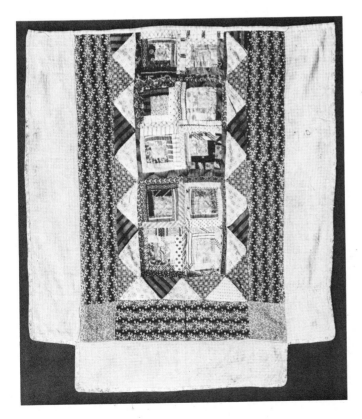

FIGURE 49. *Log Cabin doll quilt with Pyramid inner border, circa 1870. Provenance unknown. 23" × 26". Cotton. Collection of Linda Reuther, Julie Silber/Mary Strickler's Quilt Collection.*

A single man with an axe could secure for himself and his family protection against the natural elements that sought to defeat him. The self-reliance and self-sufficiency of American settlers and pioneers were qualities assigned to the formation of the American character, and the Log Cabin became a visual symbol for these American attributes.

As her father and brother constructed the simple, sturdy shelter that might house generations after her, a young girl at her mother's knee would work her own Log Cabin (Figure 49). It became the quintessential American quilt. As the father erected the outside shelter of roughest woods, the mother would work her own soft shelter for her children, and the construction of both cabin and block is remarkably similar. As the cabin was set on a foundation of stones, the quilt block itself was also affixed to a firm foundation, in this case a muslin block. The hearth, last to be installed in the cabin, was the first to be affixed to the quilt block, and around that base—the center of the home around which the family gathered and children worked and played—logs of fabric were constructed. With slight variations in their color

FIGURE 50. *Log Cabin, Courthouse Steps variation, circa 1880. Lancaster County, Pennsylvania. 40¼″ × 41″. Cotton. Collection of Marilyn and Ron Kowaleski.*

and placement, the blocks she worked into the classical arrangements of her Log Cabin quilts were visual abstractions of life on the American frontier.

A Pennsylvania quiltmaker chose to concentrate on the expansion of the borders of single blocks into two small sister quilts (Figures 50 and 51), but in most instances blocks were joined to each other to present graphic elements as clearly defined as the circumstances of the child's life. Windmill Blades (Figure 52 and Plate 47) and Straight Furrow (Figure 53 and Plate 55) acknowledged the family's dependence on the earth and the elements; Barn Raising (Figure 54 and Plate 59) and Courthouse Steps (Plate 53) established the dependency upon even remote segments of community. But essentially, they were dependent upon themselves, and there was perhaps no time in the history of the United States when the family unit was of such importance. Each family unit had to be self-sustaining, children often providing that extra measure of physical labor that meant survival itself. The standard Log Cabin pattern is one of four blocks turned inward and worked across the quilt (Plate 48), the light and

FIGURE 51. *Log Cabin with Carpenter's Wheel center block, circa 1880. Lancaster County, Pennsylvania. 43³/₄" × 45¹/₂". Cotton. Collection of Linda Reuther, Julie Silber/Mary Strickler's Quilt Collection.*

dark patterns of the diagonals offering a suggestion of those wilderness dwellings not unlike that described by Tocqueville:

> The whole family comes to seek shelter of an evening in the single room which it contains. This dwelling forms as it were a little world of its own. It is an ark of civilization lost in the middle of an ocean of leaves, it is sort of an oasis in the desert. A hundred paces beyond it is the everlasting forest stretching its shade around it and solitude begins again.[3]

The diaries and letters written by women who made that great westward journey suggest that the greatest sorrow might well have been the tearing away from family and friends. This now-smaller unit of affection must have been doubly precious to her.

FIGURE 52. *Log Cabin, Windmill Blades variation, circa 1870. Provenance unknown. 46" × 46". Wool and cotton. Collection of Linda and Irwin Berman.*

FIGURE 53. *Log Cabin, Straight Furrow variation, circa 1875. Lancaster County, Pennsylvania. 21" × 35¾". Cotton. Collection of Marilyn and Ron Kowaleski.*

FIGURE 54. *Log Cabin, Barn Raising variation, circa 1880. Pennsylvania.*
34³⁄₄″ × 43¹⁄₄″. Wool. Collection of Jeannette Fink.

CHAPTER
FOUR

THE IMMIGRANTS

◆◆◆

THE seventeenth-century German settlers who concentrated in southeastern Pennsylvania to participate in William Penn's great experiment brought with them not only the bitter memory of poverty and persecution, but a sweeter ethnic memory of color and design. This legacy would develop in Pennsylvania over the next two centuries into a tradition of folk art in its most purely defined form.

The traditions and techniques of old world craftsmen were carried across the Atlantic to be reworked into the American scene. As with almost all transplanted remnants of that other land, forms and designs were simplified to meet the demands of time and adapted to utilize the materials of a new physical environment. They nevertheless remained deliberately recognizable as having sprung from German roots.

One such craftsman was Daniel Pabst, a German cabinetmaker who opened his business near Second and Dock streets in Philadelphia.[1] (Appropriate to this subject, his earliest documented work and the only piece known to bear his label is a sewing box.) He acknowledged the source of his creative wellspring: "I brought all of Germany with me, in my inward eye."[2]

The traditional motifs stored in those collective "inward eyes" were translated to paper and wood, to metal and clay, and much later to the cotton quilts on the beds of Pennsylvania's children.

Such a child's first exposure to the colors and shapes of that visual heritage might well have been of *fraktur-schriften*, or *fraktur*-writing. This decorative calligraphy, embellished with the symbols we still associate with the region (tulips, hearts, distelfinks, etc.), was one of the dominant forces in the development of the visual folk traditions of Pennsylvania. Its techniques were based in the illuminated manuscripts of European religious communities. In Europe, however, printing techniques and woodblocks had increasingly displaced the need for penmanship and hand-done illustration. We see the tradition reemerge in Pennsylvania as a secular tradition.

The *fraktur* artist might have been a local schoolmaster or minister, but most often he was one of a wandering group of itinerant craftsmen. Although his work was sometimes signed, at other times we recognize a familiar hand only by identifiable individual preferences for motifs or by the geographic regions of his activities: the Flying Angel Artist, the Pseudo-Otto Artist, the Mount Pleasant Artist, the Sussel-

FIGURE 55. *Tulips with Foundation Rose, Plumes, and Swag border, circa 1875. Berks County, Pennsylvania. 42" × 42". Cotton. Collection of Rosemarie and Richard Machmer.*

Washington Artist. The limner would paint the image of the person; the *fraktur* artist would record the events of his life.

If location and finances allowed, a child's birth and baptism were recorded on a *Taufschein*. A brush of cat's hair would carry flat washes of color from homemade dyes into designs carefully outlined with a quill pen. With a flourish, the writer would enter the baby's name, its place and date of birth, the name of its parents, and any pertinent information regarding the baptism. It was not a legal document, but the recording of such history was an important element in the continually strengthening concept of family. As a baptismal gift from his godparents, the child might receive a *Geddelbriefe*, a hand-decorated paper folded around a coin. Rather than the symmetrical design associated with the *Taufschein*, here the decorative motif was simply repeated in each fold.

A Pennsylvania student's schoolmaster might prepare a *Vorschrift*, an example of handwriting made to direct and inspire the child in his own tentative attempts to master the written alphabet. Either schoolmaster or Sunday school teacher might give him a small drawing as a reward for good conduct, or diligent application to a task, or for a number of Bible verses well learned. The importance of and appreciation for even small and naive examples of these commendations is indicated by the large number that have survived, tucked away in the pages of books. As an adult, he might possess *fraktur* as decoration in the flyleaf of his Bible, or as a book mark, or house blessing, but could there ever have been greater remembered pleasure and pride than receiving beauty as a regard for fulfilling society's and family's expectations of a "good" child?

Affection and indeed passion were also expressed in a number of ways. The *Liebesbriefe* was an intricately cut love letter incorporating another German folk tradition, that of *scherenschnitte*, or scissors cutting. *Fraktur* writing further embellished the delicate paper images, which were often hearts cut from double and triple folds. The technique was also applied to children's quilts (Figures 56 and 57). The heart motif was used with restraint on quilts of other regions, but in Pennsylvania the heart was everywhere visible—not only on *fraktur*, but on blanket chests, cast-iron stoves,

FIGURE 56. *Hearts and Hexagons, circa 1890. Pennsylvania. 46" × 46". Cotton. Collection of Steve Miller American Folk Art.*

buttermolds, foot warmers, and grain bags! It therefore seems quite natural to see it in great abundance on quilts, as much an expression of joy as of sentiment.

Pennsylvania craftsmen working in all media used symbols that originated in tradition, but as the techniques moved further away from their European beginnings, so too did the meanings of those symbols stray from their original interpretations. Large painted symbols of German origin appeared bold and clear on the great red barns of Berks and Lehigh counties. Legend had assigned magical power to these "hex signs," but by 1840, when these decorations became increasingly visible in southeastern Pennsylvania, the design had become more important than its traditional definition. Many of the signs were individual efforts, the marking of the large geometrically divided circle accomplished with large compass or with chalk and string. Like the other decorative arts of the period, however, it soon became another source of income for the itinerant craftsman—and another source of design for the American pieced quilt.

The tulip is probably the most visible symbol in Pennsylvania German folk design. Like the circular configurations on those massive barns, what meaning it may have had for those early craftsmen and artists is unclear. We know that in Europe the tulip was viewed as a variation of the Holy Lily, its three petals symbolic of the Trinity. But it was realism rather than religion that saw it drawn in such numbers throughout the Pennsylvania valleys.

After its introduction to Europe from Asia Minor in the middle of the sixteenth century, the tulip became the flower

FIGURE 57. *Double Hearts, circa 1890. Pennsylvania. 34" × 43". Cotton. Collection of Felicia Melero Holtzinger.*

of fashion. *Tulipenwuth* (tulip-madness) swept the continent as huge fortunes were made and lost with the buying and selling of bulbs. In the eighteenth century, the use of the tulip as a decorative motif on the slip- and sgraffito-decorated earthenware was pervasive throughout the pottery of Germany's Palatinate Valley. Surely it was a design and skill brought to Pennsylvania by the potters from that region who were very likely among the waves of immigrants. The simple shape of the tulip made it adaptable to all material and put it within the creative capacity of even the most untrained hands. Both flower and image flourished in Pennsylvania (Figure 55).

But prior to 1850, the Pennsylvania *Hausfrau's* featherbeds generally displayed the product of the weaver's loom rather than the quilter's frame. In 1683, Daniel Pastorius and his group of German weavers arrived in Germantown, and the weaving industry flourished. The woven coverlet was a symbol of pride in the tradition of excellence that was established. Rather than templates passed from mother to daughter, patterns books were passed from father to son.

In the history of American quilts, those of Pennsylvania German design came late, but when they came it was with form and color worked in such exuberance and individuality that on visual criteria alone their provenance is often the easiest to establish. The bright reds, greens, and yellows selected by Edna E. Meyer (Figure 58) were often joined by oranges and pinks, certainly not the subdued tones favored by the Edwardian ladies under the guidance of *Godey's Lady's Books*. The simple, direct statement of both color and design seems a logical reflection of the character and background of the Pennsylvania German quiltmaker.

The nineteenth century brought the American quilt to its fullest expression, but the last years of that century were touched by the creative damage done by the Industrial Revolution. There had, much earlier, begun an imperceptible but irreversible decline in the work of the hand.

In Lancaster County, Pennsylvania, at almost that same moment in time, a new quilt began to emerge. From the plainest of people, simple and intense graphic design moved from grays and browns into a brilliant burst of magenta,

FIGURE 58. *Sawtooth Diamond with flowers and stars, 1881. Quiltmaker: Edna E. Meyer (signed and dated). Lebanon County, Pennsylvania. 48¼" × 48¼". Cotton. Collection of Dr. and Mrs. Donald M. Herr.*

blue, and green. This new quilt flourished for a few decades, was translated, diluted, and then—in its most classic form— disappeared forever. This was the quilt of the Amish, a group whose religion had set them deliberately apart from the "English" society. Their community was then almost as we see it now—plain, devout, agrarian, and separate.

The principles (the *Ordnung*) that direct the life of the Amish are an oral tradition, and the beginnings of those magnificent quilts are lost somewhere in that group memory. Rather than document the development of the Amish quilt-maker, we can only consider the glorious fruits of her labor.

For the Pennsylvania German quiltmaker not bound by religious restraints, we have seen that the symbols and motifs of her European origins were everywhere visible around her. Drawing on those motifs, her quilt was the result of personal choices—techniques and patterns presented excit-ing and almost unlimited possibilities. For the Amish quilt-maker, such choices were not hers alone to make. The Amish quilt represents not what was possible for the individual, but what was acceptable to the group. By tradition born of religious direction, the Amish quiltmaker approached the making of her quilt with a given set of absolutes. Rather than expand her creative boundaries, those boundaries had been set, firm and inflexible, by a community that rejected the worldly, the fancy, the vain. The Amish quilt is a reflection of passion restrained.

Within those rigid boundaries, however, the quiltmaker could concentrate with singular focus on wonderful color and infinitesimal stitch. The classic Lancaster Amish quilt began at a point of specified simplicity. Large pieces of wool, highly receptive to homemade dyes, were worked into large primary shapes—squares and rectangles predominating. The wide surfaces, simple and calm, waited to receive the limited number of creative responsibilities the quiltmaker felt free to exercise. Color and stitch—those creative alternatives were narrow, but they were largely her own.

Appliqué being a technique considered too fancy, the tulip, the rose, the running vine border—those exuberant shapes in bright red, yellow, green, and white that identify so many other Pennsylvania quilts—find form on the Amish

FIGURE 59. *Nine-patch medallion with multiple borders, circa 1880. Amish. Lancaster County, Pennsylvania. 49" × 49". Wool and cotton. Collection of Linda and Irwin Berman.*

quilt only in small quilted stitches. Quilting with dark thread on the plain surfaces, the Amish quiltmaker built an enormously diverse linear pattern. Some of those patterns must have on occasion skirted the border of what was acceptable. We can see in her elaborate quilted patterns some of the emotional enthusiasm the maker may have been denied in other areas of her life.

As quiltmaking flouished in other Amish communities, slight regional differences became more defined, such as the preoccupation with the nine-patch in the Mifflin County quilts made by the Nebraska Amish. But wherever they were worked, all the Amish sensibilities moved firmly from large quilt to small. The Amish child was born into a life of specific boundaries and defined expectation, and those were the qualities of his childhood quilts.

CHAPTER
FIVE

THE NATION

◆◆◆

WE see in the design of many small quilts emotional and aesthetic ties to other places and other times; but in the nineteenth century they began to chronicle the political and patriotic development of the nation. In both country and quilts, traditions merged to form something shiny and new, strengthened by the diverse elements from which they were formed.

A new nation is required to adorn itself with new symbols, images meant to define and to inspire. None of these resultant symbols seem to have been considered inappropriate for the quilts of the youngest citizens, who often slept wrapped in suggestions of Old Glory herself (Figure 60). As the country had once been the hope for the father, the child was now the hope for the country, and the quilt its mother worked was often a reminder of both promise and obligation. The Kansas baby who slept beneath these stars and stripes (Figure 61) was one with the symbol; both were indispensable to the strength and continuity of the nation.

Two small doll quilts (Figure 62) illustrate the changing visual characteristics of America's flags, the symbol seemingly most capable of evoking patriotic fervor. The Stars and

Stripes are reworked from a bit of the bunting that draped the countryside during nineteenth-century political campaigns. The Bars quilt, however, may have been intended to recall a more subtle expression of patriotism. In most colonial towns, respectable citizens often joined a secret patriotic society called the Sons of Liberty. While the "Liberty" flags of other groups displayed that stirring ideal through the use of the written word, the flag used by the Sons of Liberty was one of implication rather than of observation. Its ground was composed of nine vertical red and white sripes. The number of stripes was derived from $4/5$, this in turn suggesting "Number 45," the famous pamphlet in which the Englishman John Wilkes gave impetus to

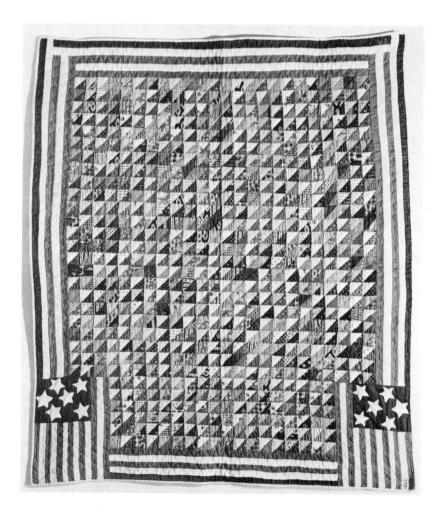

FIGURE 60. *Birds-in-the-Air with flag corners, 1862 (dated). Pennsylvania. 36" × 43½". Cotton. Private collection.* Photograph courtesy of America Hurrah Antiques

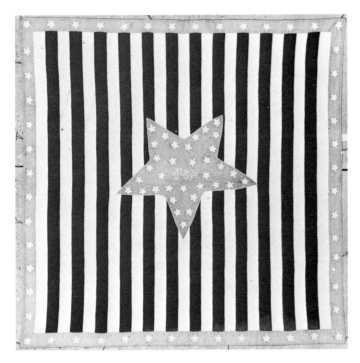

the Revolution.[1] The number nine came to have special meaning: nine states had been the first to ratify the Constitution; the first rattlesnake ("Don't Tread on Me") appeared in the *Philadelphia Gazette* divided into nine sections, with the head representing all of the New England states. The nine red and white stripes on this doll quilt remind us of a Revolution conceived in secrecy—the bunting that decorated the open political activities of a democracy is the harvest it reaped.

The requirements for a symbol are, of course, that it appear in great profusion in a number of media and that its meaning is clear and continuing. The American bald eagle was selected on June 20, 1782, by the Continental Congress as our national symbol, its placement on the Great Seal of the United States the culmination of a six-year search and debate. Its image was soon everywhere within sight of young and impressionable eyes—carved, painted, stamped, molded, incised, printed, and sewn.

The selection of the eagle as our national symbol was met with overwhelming popular approval although some dissent was noted. (Benjamin Franklin considered the eagle to be

FIGURE 62. Left: *Bars doll quilt, circa 1850. Pennsylvania. 12½" × 14¾". Cotton. Collection of Kiracofe and Kile.* Right: *Stars and Stripes doll quilt, circa 1876. Provenance unknown. 12½" × 15¼". Cotton. Collection of Kiracofe and Kile.*

"a bird of bad moral character," and Nathaniel Hawthorne, observing the great carved bird at the Salem Custom House, noted "the customary infirmity of temperament that characterizes this unhappy fowl."[2]) To the general populace, however, it was celebrated as a glorious and inspired choice.

The English were well aware of the American preference for fabrics bearing the symbols of national identity. The piece of whole-cloth forming the center panel in Plate 1 is a section of "Eagle and Shield from Seal of the United States," an immensely popular fabric roller-printed in Manchester, England, for export to the American market. The pattern was printed in red and black on a variety of colored grounds. Its commercial success is indicated by the large number of pieces and fragments that survive.

In a variety of forms and stances, the eagle was appliquéd onto American quilts throughout the nineteenth century. In its most extravagant application, it appeared as a favored motif on the magnificent Album Quilts worked by the ladies of Baltimore: on a quilt made by his friends for Benjamin

Foard of Folk, Baltimore County;[3] on a Bride's Quilt made for Miss Isabella Batty on the occasion of her marriage to Mr. Andrew Crow, October 12, 1852;[4] on a Freedom Quilt given to Benjamin Almoney in 1845 on his twenty-first birthday;[5] and on a quilt worked in 1843 by Sophia Bankard Whitaker for her own pleasure.[6]

Someone else worked a classic Baltimore Eagle block during that same period: the body is a bright blue traditional rainbow or fondu print, the teardrop shapes appear on wing and tail feathers and above its talons, it holds in its beak a delicate bow and floral ribbons all joining other elements of design and technique to establish its provenance. This particular eagle and the sprays it holds (excluding the bow) are almost identical to one in a full Album Quilt made for Samuel Williams, 1846–1847.[7] The patriotic symbols and single floral spray it holds in its grasp are identical (but

FIGURE 63. *Baltimore Album Quilt with Zigzag border, circa 1850. Maryland. 36" × 50". Cotton. Private collection.* Courtesy of Richard Opfer

reversed) to another.[8] The recipient of this splendid block (surely not its maker!) unfortunately sacrificed sensitivity to sentiment and trimmed all four sides of the block to fit a set of five other somewhat less distinguished offerings (Figure 63).

The scissors have, on the left of the block, severed another patriotic emblem, a Liberty Cap hanging from a Liberty Pole. These long poles were put up in town squares to symbolize the Liberty Tree under which the Sons of Liberty met and from whose branches officials of the British government were often hung in effigy. The Liberty Cap itself was a kind of drooping stocking cap worn in classical times by liberated slaves and appearing in that same connotation during the French Revolution.

The Liberty Cap and Pole appear (as does the Liberty Bell) on a piece of cotton fabric printed to simulate pieced calico. Such simulated fabric became popular in the middle of the nineteenth century, and the technique was used to design the centennial fabric that is used in this whole-cloth quilt, worked to add patriotic adornment to a doll's four-poster bed (Figure 64).

Pole and Cap are often held, or Liberty Cap worn, by Miss Liberty (sometimes called Columbia). An English copperplate printed around 1875 for export to the former colonies is titled "Apotheosis of Benjamin Franklin and George Wash-

FIGURE 64. *Whole-cloth doll quilt, circa 1876. Provenance unknown. 12" × 12". Cotton (a Centennial fabric printed to simulate pieced work). Collection of Daughters of the American Revolution Museum.*

FIGURE 65. *Miss Liberty, Eagle, and Shield (detail, Storybook Quilt), circa 1890. See Plate 49. Quiltmaker: Eudotia Sturgis Wilcox. Provenance unknown. 68″ × 78¼″. Predominantly silk and velvet. Western History Collection, Natural History Museum of Los Angeles County.*

ington." It shows Miss Liberty with the Pole and Cap in her right hand. Her left hand (with Mr. Franklin's assistance) holds aloft a banner reading "WHERE LIBERTY DWELLS THERE IS MY COUNTRY."

Miss Liberty evolved through a number of forms, beginning as a bare-breasted Indian Amazon and softening into a more romantic and classical figure. She is usually accompanied by one or more of our national symbols, such as the shield seen here (Figure 65). The hint of the eagle to her right is elaborated in silk, velvet, and ribbon in the top right corner of this ambitious Crazy Quilt (Plate 49).

Silk political ribbons appeared at the beginning of the century. Most often intended for use as bookmarks, they also found their way from a box of treasured souvenirs onto the elaborate Crazy Quilt thrown across a sofa in the fashionable Victorian parlor. Silk, because of its fragile nature, was seldom used for a child's quilt, and only a few examples have survived. Four campaign ribbons have been incorporated into a quilt of simple pieced-silk blocks to form a central medallion that is a unique record of political loyalties (Figure 66). Henry Clay, a dominant figure in American politics for decades following the War of 1812, spent a lifetime unsuccessfully pursuing the presidency. The ribbons worked into this quilt speak of his final efforts. The top and bottom ribbons bear legends and drawings:

Young Men's
National Whig Convention
of Ratification
(drawing of an eagle)
Henry Clay
(drawing of Clay)
"Mind Your Business"
(drawing of farmer with plow and horses)
The Ashland Farm
Baltimore, May 2, 1841

The ribbons on the left and right bear a portrait of Clay beneath a drawing of an eagle, followed by the inscription:

Henry Clay
Whig
National Convention
May 2, 1841

The inclusion of these ribbons is appropriate and understandable considering that the quilt was made to cover a baby born into a political family (its mother was the niece of the governor of Iowa). If we need a less biased example of the inclusion of political material in children's quilts, we can consider a piece of less refinement (Figure 31). Two political bandannas are set with a variety of children's handkerchiefs. Both were used during the 1884 campaign for the presidency and they are identical in design except for the candidates' names and portraits. The American eagle is at the top of each piece, hovering over "The Constitution" and a pair of

FIGURE 66. *Center panel of political ribbons with Broken Dishes and Pyramid borders, circa 1845. Quiltmaker: Julia Kirkwood Godfrey, niece of Iowa's Governor Samuel Kirkwood. Baltimore, Maryland. 30½" × 34". Silk. Collection of Linda and Irwin Berman.*

clasped hands. The bandanna on the left bears the legends:

For President	For Vice President
Grover Cleveland	Thomas A. Hendricks
of	of
New York	Indiana

beneath their respective portraits. The bandanna on the right bears the portraits and identification of James G. Blaine of Maine and John A. Logan of Illinois, candidates for those same offices. The inclusion of this political memorabilia seems a natural addition to the other activities of childhood.

The symbols on these small quilts were not intended merely for amusement or passive observation. They were meant to inspire interest and, eventually, active participation in the affairs of the state. Liberty had been hard won and was yet to be nurtured and protected.

The symbols of the Republic and the political fervor they evoked were drawn together in that grand American spectacle, the political parade. What child could resist this tangible tradition of the democratic process?

> Simple homemade torchlights gave way to mass-produced torchlights, which were sometimes artfully shaped into imaginative designs. There were hand-held glass lanterns, paper Japanese lanterns, parade canes, wooden spears and shields, and whistles and other noisemakers. In 1888, the peak year for torchlight parades, a parade could easily last two or three hours; it often began or ended with a spectacular fireworks display. Miniature cannon up to three feet in length sounded highly satisfying reports and volcano tubes and wagons showered streams of sparks onto marchers and spectators alike. Other wagons, suitably decorated in bunting and banners carried local dignitaries or perhaps one of those marvelous cornet bands that were so popular in the 1880's and 1890's . . . riding high above it all were plain and fancy banners brightly illuminated by the light of a thousand torches. Among the marchers in a torchlight parade would be boys too young to vote who were paid a few cents to carry a torch.[9]

These magnificent displays, often the major event of the year in a rural community, were carefully orchestrated promotions for politicians and for the issues of the day, and those issues were deemed appropriate for a child's consideration. A popular cotton printed fabric, "Honor to the Laboring Classes," was worked into a whole-cloth doll quilt (Figure 67). Floral wreaths surround pictorial tributes: "Labor Is Honorable," "Honor to the Iron Worker," "The Two Powers in Accord," and "After Work the Happy Home." Appropriately, it was quilted on a sewing machine!

Moral issues were as passionately political as were economic theories. When "Drunkard's Path" was used as a pattern for a child's quilt, it is too often suggested that it would, in that

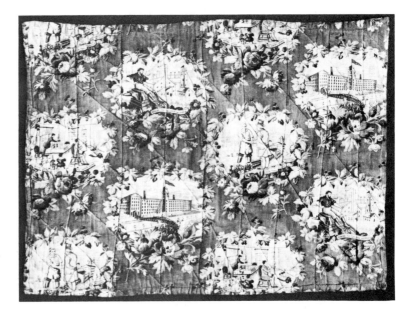

FIGURE 67. *Whole-cloth doll quilt, "Honor to the Laboring Classes," circa 1875. Provenance unknown. 22¾" × 16¾". Cotton. Collection of The Baltimore Museum of Art, gift of Dena S. Katzenberg.*

instance, surely have been called by another name. In the spirit of the times, however, it would easily have been a deliberate and meaningful choice.

With Massachusetts and the Methodists leading the way, temperance groups became active even before the beginning of the nineteenth century. Their moral indignation and activity rose to a fever pitch in the 1840s, a period in which America was concentrating on perfecting its social institutions. Mass meetings featured reformed inebriates moving a crowd to tears with excessively sentimental accounts of personal degradation and redemption. Women rampaged through shops and taverns seeking to halt the dispensing of the odious brew. If they themselves had not suffered first-hand the personal tragedy wrought by John Barleycorn, they could nevertheless be moved to action by the hundreds of woeful tales and tracts spewing forth from New England presses and in temperance novels, a literary genre then much in vogue.

In 1836, children themselves were actively recruited for the great battle when Reverend Thomas Hunt founded the Cold Water Army. The first of a number of juvenile temperance groups active in the nineteenth century, it is estimated that hundreds of thousands of eager children took its pledge:

We, Cold Water Girls and Boys,
Freely renounce the treacherous joy
of Brandy, Whiskey, Rum and Gin;
The Serpent's lure to death and sin:
Wine, Beer and Cider we detest,
And thus we'll make our parents blest;
So here we pledge perpetual hate
To all that can intoxicate.

As the movement began to press for outright prohibition rather than merely temperance, cold water was advocated as a desirable substitute and the children of the Cold Water Army proudly wore white satin ribbons featuring a picture of a fountain.

Although the movement was always strongest in rural America, it was a national political issue. By mid-century, however, the dissension between those who favored self-control in the question of drink and those who were in favor of legal restraint began diverting the energies of the cause from a single purpose. This fact, and the shadow of the approaching Civil War, caused the intensity of the movement to slacken somewhat. Still, President Rutherford B. Hayes's wife, "Lemonade Lucy," banned alcohol from the White House, and even at formal dinners the guests were served fruit juice or cold water. Perhaps she had once worn that satin ribbon while marching for teetotalism in a small "Band of Hope."

The women who worked America's quilts were often forced to express their political views through the sewing box rather than the ballot box. And just as political cartoonists exerted immense influence on the subject of prohibition, so too did the quiltmaker continue to produce her Drunkard's Path.

The mother who covered her child with a Drunkard's Path (Figure 68) need not have considered the pattern to be an eventual enticement to follow that sorrowful road, but rather a subliminal invitation to one day join her in the great cause to be won—and lost—in the next century.

There was yet another issue being addressed, with important parallels to the temperance movement. Antislavery societies had held twenty-four joint conventions between

1794 and 1829. Some were content simply to refrain from individual participation in the evils of slavery; for others, the only acceptable solution was the total and immediate abolition of slavery in America.

The subject had been interpreted on an eighteenth-century fabric, two strips of which have been pieced together to form the backing on a child's quilt (Figure 69). It is typical of the French toile so fashionable at the time—monochromatic in color, pictorial in theme. A white man stands beneath palm trees negotiating with a black in loose, western dress, gesturing toward tall-masted sailing ships waiting in the harbor.

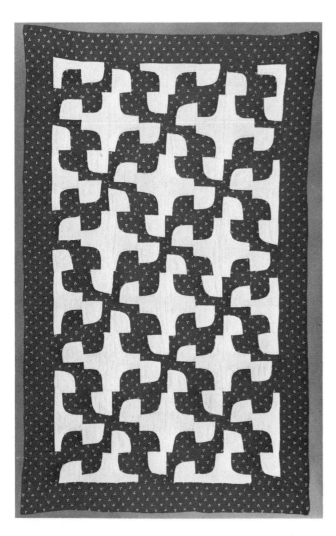

FIGURE 68. *Drunkard's Path, circa 1880. Provenance unknown. 27″ × 44″. Cotton. Collection of Glendora Hutson.*

A weeping black man sits in chains in a rowboat while another stands between two whites, one of whom holds aloft a large stick. This tableau is watched by a black mother and child who cling together. Another black woman (one baby strapped to her back, another at her feet) attends to a white woman and child reclining in classical pose. It is a romantic rendering of harsh realities.

That blue and white narrative was written in black and white in a number of abolitionist publications. *The Philanthropist* appeared in Ohio in 1817, and in 1829 a pamphlet, *Walker's Appeal*, was distributed among southern blacks. In 1831, a Boston reformer, William Lloyd Garrison, began to publish *The Liberator*, and his first issue set forth the unconditional intent of both publisher and paper: ". . . urge me not to use moderation in a cause like the present. I am in

FIGURE 69. *Backing, Figure 73. Unidentified slavery toile.*

earnest—I will not equivocate—I will not excuse—I will not retreat a single inch—*and I will be heard.*"

And heard he was, in North and South, by men and women—and by American's children. The abolitionist societies welcomed juvenile participation, just as the temperance groups did, and separate and auxiliary groups were formed especially to encourage the efforts of those youthful zealots.

It is extremely rare to have journalistic documentation of a particular quilt, but on the impassioned pages of Garrison's weekly paper, a detailed account of the purpose and circumstances of one such early quilt does in fact exist. From the January 2, 1837, edition of *The Liberator*:

The Ladies Fair

The proposed Anti-Slavery Fair was held on Thursday, the 22nd of December. The choice of that day was accidental; but it was a pleasant and appropriate manner of celebrating the anniversary of the Pilgrims. The convenient and well lighted hall, called the Artist's Gallery, was duly prepared for our reception, and we had not the slightest reason to complain of reluctance or want of courtesy on the part of the proprietor. The hall was filled with visitors at an early hour, and continued full until late in the evening. Very many of these were not Abolition*ists*, but belonged to a large and increasing class of community, who have been Abolution*ized* by Anti-Slavery efforts. Not a few of the wives and daughters of 'gentlemen of property and standing' were among the purchasers. A piece of the old oak of the *Constitution* was offered for sale; and we regretted that we had not placed beside it the relics of the *anti-slavery sign*, destroyed by a patrician mob in 1834.

Around the hall was placed in large letters the motto: 'On this day did our Fathers *land* on the Rock of Freedom; let us *stand* firmly on this Rock.'

The cake-table was loaded with varieties of cake, made of sugar, not manufactured by slaves, and near it was placed a motto, Free Labor. One of our friends sent a jar of deliciously fresh Grapes and a dozen pomegranates, accompanied by a very pleasant note, expressing the hope that 'the enslaved children of Africa might soon be enabled to sit under their own vine and fig-tree, with none to molest or make them afraid.'

There was great variety in the articles, and many of them were very handsome and tasteful. The ladies have ever regarded the pecuniary benefit derived from these sales as but *one* of several reasons in their favor. The main object is to keep the subject before the public eye, and by every innocent expedient to promote perpetual discussion. We wish to bring Truth and Falsehood in continual *juxtaposition*, for we know full well that 'truth never came off the worse in a fair and open encounter.'

To promote this favorite object, various mottoes and devices were stamped upon the articles offered for sale. Bunches of quills bore the label, 'Twenty-five Weapons for Abolitionists.' On the wafer boxes was written, 'The doom of Slavery is *sealed*.' On one side of the pen-wipers was inscribed, 'Wipe out the blot of Slavery'; on the other, 'Plead the cause with thy Pen.' On some needle-books was printed, 'May the use of our needles prick the consciences of slaveholders'; others were made in the form of small shoes, and on the soles was written, 'Trample not on the Oppressed.' Some watch cases bore the inscription, 'The political economist counts time by years, the suffering slave reckons it by *minutes*'; on others was written, 'The greatest friend of Truth is *Time*, her greatest enemy is prejudice.' Small silken bags of pefume, for bureau drawers, bore the motto, 'The kingdom of Heaven is like unto leaven, which a *woman* hid in three measures of meal, until the whole was leavened.' The iron-holders were marked, 'Anti-Slave *holders*.' Small hearts cut from a knot of white oak were called

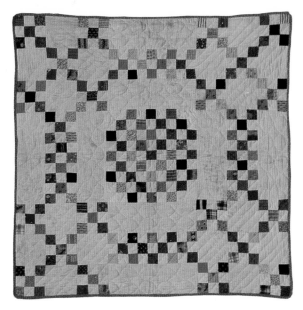

PLATE 27. *Puss in the Corner, circa 1880. Pennsylvania. 27¼" × 27½". Cotton. Collection of Marilyn and Ron Kowaleski.*

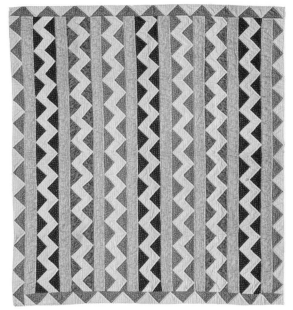

PLATE 28. *Streak of Lightning with Pyramid border, circa 1885. Pennsylvania. 34" × 36". Cotton. Collection of Marilyn and Ron Kowaleski.*

PLATE 29. *Philadelphia Pavement, circa 1890. Farmersville, Pennsylvania. 37" × 37". Cotton. Collection of Smith and Wanda Johnson.*

PLATE 30. *Postage Stamp Four-patch variation, circa 1875. New York State. 38" × 38". Cotton. Private collection.* Photograph courtesy of America Hurrah Antiques

PLATE 38. *Buds and Leaves with Swag and Tassel border, circa 1870. Provenance unknown. 36½″ × 37½″. Cotton. Collection of Phyllis Haders.*

PLATE 39. *Irish Chain with appliquéd motifs and pieced initials, I. E. C., circa 1880. Made for Ida Euretta Cole. Hillsdale, New York. 52¼″ × 62″. Cotton. Collection of Marie Michal and Peter Lubalin.* Courtesy of Guernsey's Auction

PLATE 40. *Double Hearts with Bird, Child, and Baby Hands, circa 1855. Possibly Connecticut. 36½″ × 38½″. Cotton. Collection of America Hurrah Antiques.*

PLATE 42. *Original design, circa 1850. Indiana. 42½″ × 43″. Cotton. Collection of Jackie and Stanley Schneider.*

PLATE 41. *Love Apple variation with Running Vine border, circa 1876. Provenance unknown. 46″ × 58″. Cotton. Collection of America Hurrah Antiques.*

PLATE 43. *Cherry Wreath with Swag and Bow border, circa 1875. Mechanicsburg, Pennsylvania. 25″ × 27″. Cotton. Machine quilted. Collection of Felicia Melero Holtzinger.*

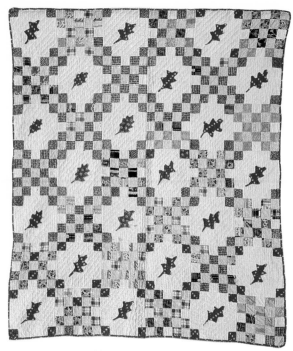

PLATE 44. *Double Irish Chain with Oak Leaf, circa 1870. Provenance unknown. 34″ × 39″. Cotton. Collection of Linda Reuther, Julie Silber/Mary Strickler's Quilt Collection.*

PLATE 45. *Log Cabin with Courthouse Steps variation and Pyramid border, circa 1875. Provenance unknown. 30¼″ × 42¾″. Cotton. Collection of B. J. Welden.* **Courtesy of Edward Brown.**

PLATE 46. Left: *Log Cabin, Straight Furrow variation doll quilt, circa 1880. York County, Pennsylvania. 14¾″ × 17¾″. Cotton. Collection of Smith and Wanda Johnson.* Middle: *Log Cabin, Barn Raising variation doll quilt, circa 1875. Berks County, Pennsylvania. 18¼″ × 18¼″. Cotton and wool. Collection of Smith and Wanda Johnson.* Right: *Log Cabin, Courthouse Steps variation doll quilt, circa 1880. Lancster County, Pennsylvania. 15¾″ × 17″. Cotton. Collection of Evie Gleason.*

PLATE 47. *Windmill Blades, circa 1870. Pennsylvania. 51" × 51". Cotton. Collection of Dr. and Mrs. Roger Lerner.*

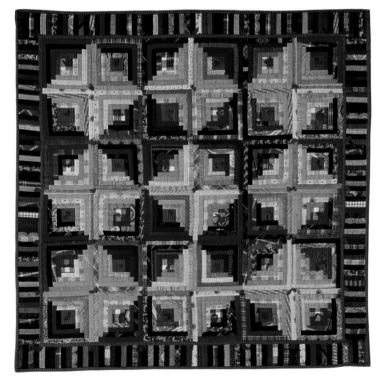

PLATE 48. *Log Cabin with striped border, circa 1895. Lancaster County, Pennsylvania. 37" × 37½". Cotton. Collection of Marilyn and Ron Kowaleski.*

PLATE 49. *Storybook Crazy Quilt, circa 1890. See Figures 6, 37, 38 and 65. Quiltmaker: Eudotia Sturgis Wilcox. Provenance unknown. 68″ × 78¼″. Predominantly silk and velvet. Western History Collection, Natural History Museum of Los Angeles County.*

'Hearts of Oak' for Abolitionists. A cradle-quilt was made of patchwork in small stars; and on the central star was written with indelible ink:

> *'Mother! When around your child*
> *You clasp your arms in love,*
> *And when with grateful joy you raise*
> *Your eyes to God above—*
> *Think of the Negro-mother*
> *When her child is torn away—*
> Sold for a little slave—oh, then,
> For *that* poor mother pray!'*[10.]*

FIGURE 70. *Evening Star (detail, Antislavery quilt), 1836. Massachusetts. 36" × 46". Cotton. Collection of the Society for the Preservation of New England Antiquities.*

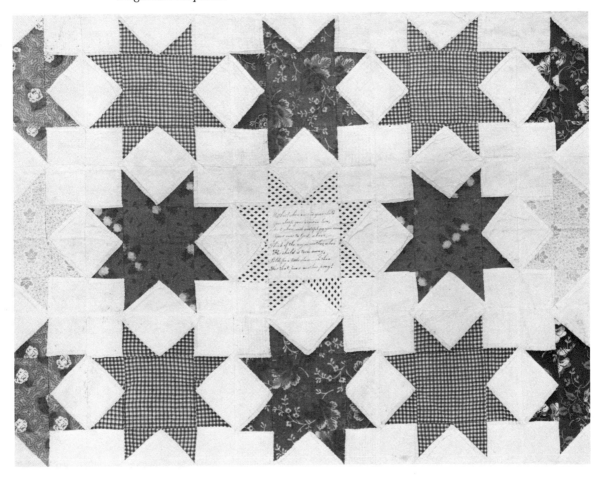

FIGURE 71. *Antislavery quilt, circa 1860. Quiltmaker: Maria Theresa Baldwin Hollander, daughter of Col. Charles North Baldwin. Exhibited in New York. 43″ × 43¾″. Silk. Privately owned.* Photograph courtesy of the Society for the Preservation of New England Antiquities

The quilt purchased that December evening was soft and simple, but its sturdy stitches and strong purpose have somehow kept it safe for almost a century and a half (Figure 70).

The Ladies Fair was a financial success. When the proceeds were counted, the total sum raised (including a $25.61 contribution by the Juvenile Anti-Slavery Sewing Circle) was $550, and ". . . the next morning, the ladies paid all that remained of their pledge of one thousand dollars to the Massachusetts society."[11] The moral returns were still to be determined.

For the children who had attended, there was ". . . candy, and various other articles of confectionary . . ." wrapped in paper, on which were printed the following verses:

> *Come, little ones! For the sweets ye see,*
> *Were made by the labor of the free;*
> *And freely to-day ye may partake,*
> *Even for the toil-worn bondman's sake;*
>
> *For the price you pay perchance may save*
> *From the cruel scourge some tortured slave:*
> *(Your friends will explain how a single cent*
> *May cause the steeled heart to relent.)*
>
> *And year after year, as Christmas comes,*
> *With its papers of pleasant sugar-plums,*
> *Ever be careful to enquire*
> *Respecting the fact of the laborer's hire.*[12]

Many of the children who bought that penny candy lived to see the result of the messages in which it was wrapped: the payment may even have been their own dear sons.

In the 1860s, as that terrible war approached, Maria Theresa Baldwin Hollander, daughter of Col. Charles North Baldwin, exhibited an elegant child's quilt in New York (Figure 71). In the center she had worked in silk floss the most moving of our national symbols—the eagle and flag of the Republic. As her strongest emotional weapon, she invoked the image and the name of George Washington:

State linked to State—Oh! Unity Divine!
Our cherished Washington! The praise be thine.
And yet, alas! by thee, regarded not,
One curse remains—a monstrous, hideous blot.
But should thy spirit in a new form burst forth,
The stain to 'rase that tarnishes the South;
This proferred Quilt would proudly claim to be
Spread o'er the cradle of his infancy.

In 1789, George Washington had toured in triumph through the thirteen states of the new Republic. In many areas, his countrymen had honored him by scratching the outline of an eagle in whitewash newly applied to their front windows, behind which a lighted candle had been placed to illuminate the design. Here Washington (whose popularity as a national hero was often translated into a symbol for the country itself) and the eagle are joined again, this time linking the thirty-one states noted in the embroidered stars. Washington and the Eagle, symbols used to draw small towns and villages into one great nation, were rejoined in this small quilt in a plea for the perfection of that union.

In the verse worked by the quiltmaker, her expressed hope for Washington's reincarnation in a new, small, determined spirit is compatible with the temper of the times. If this was to be a perfect nation, the children were considered to be the instruments of that perfection. That spirit was unborn and the quilt never used; the links were broken one by one, only later to be reforged at a cost no one could have imagined.

The Quilts

FIGURE 72. *Palampore whole-cloth doll quilt, circa 1800. New England.
17½" × 25". Cotton. Collection of Kiracofe and Kile.*

CHAPTER
SIX

THE CLOTH

◆◆◆

NINETEENTH-century quilts and quiltmakers—these were truly
the fabric of the nation. It is from the tale of homespun and
store-bought that we can also weave the history of America.

In the centuries preceding the Industrial Revolution, there
was an importance attached to textiles that is almost impossible for the contemporary observer to assess or understand.
Household inventories of the seventeenth and eighteenth
centuries consistently listed them prominently and in detail.
Any imported cloth was purchased at great expense, and
whenever a woman lived away from a seaport, the fabric she
used for her household linen and her family's clothing was
most often the product of her own labor. The piece of fabric
bought not with money but with the work of her waking
hours was something to view with special respect. Each inch
was tangible proof of the extent of her efforts.

For the first pioneers, the production of homespun was a
necessity and was of a rough and utilitarian nature, for the
struggle at hand was one of simple survival. Home manufactures would suffice when there was shelter to be secured
and a garden to be planted.

Once the foothold of civilization was established, the

wealthy in Virginia, Georgia, and the Carolinas reinforced their ties to European wealth and goods. This small doll quilt (Figure 72), possibly eighteenth century, is a tender testament to the importation of chintz that was the fashion in England and therefore the vogue in America. But for the less privileged, and for those who were about the business of expanding the nation's boundaries, the production of homespun continued apace, and did so, for a variety of reasons, well into the second half of the nineteenth century.

In the middle of the seventeenth century, it was labor by decree. Colonial Massachusetts authorities required that flax be grown and that both young boys and girls be taught to spin it into linen thread to meet the quotas that were to be assigned each family. Children of the poor and orphans were placed in workhouses to card and to spin.
be grown and that both young boys and girls be taught to weave it into linen thread to meet the quotas that were to be assigned each family. Children of the poor and orphans were placed in workhouses to card and to spin.

In the latter part of the eighteenth century, the use of child labor was viewed as both a positive and patriotic act. England's 1765 passage of the Stamp Act initiated an increased community effort in the production of home-manufactured textiles. Self-sufficiency in that area was considered a matter of high priority.

By the next century, children were at the great machines that were building America's ever-expanding textile industry. Political independence from England had come at a great cost. A considerable portion of the price of economic independence was being paid by the smallest citizens. These were the children to whom the celebration of childhood was denied. Elizabeth Barrett Browning wrote:

> *The young, young children, O my brothers,*
> *They are weeping bitterly;*
> *They are weeping in the playtime of others*
> *In the land of the free.*

But beyond duty to the nation, it was the goal of each family to establish self-sufficiency, a goal of particular necessity for families on the frontier. The participation of children in the multiple tasks associated with the production of those home manufactures was considered an economic advantage; but it also reinforced the concept of that family as a unit, one in which each must perform individually for the good of the whole.

Eventually, the great eastern rivers were harnessed, and American manufacturers were making store-bought a possibility even for those of the less-privileged class. Improved transportation increasingly allowed peddlers and wagons to carry calico into otherwise isolated areas. But one should not assume that the establishment of America's textile industry meant creative choices for all of the nineteenth-century quiltmakers. It did not touch, to any meaningful degree, the woman who had already moved on farther West, where road returned to trail.

As the quiltmaker stepped once again into uncleared forests, it was of little consequence that glorious fabrics were available to the mother and sister she had left behind. The first priorities of the woman in a log cabin beyond the Mississippi, or in a sod house on the prairie, were the same as those set by women settling the rocky shores of the Atlantic almost two centuries before. There was a home to be built, a garden to be planted, and then perhaps time for the memories to be pulled from a piece-bag. Even when curtains had been hung, the first crop safely harvested, and perhaps a small sum set aside to pay for a bit of bright blue calico, there were often few opportunities for the frontier woman to find any of the factory-made woven wealth. This was a pattern repeated with the opening of each new frontier, where new quilts depended on ingenuity and the ability to make do.

In many instances, making do carried with it special social and political implications. In 1768, as an expression of patriotic idealism, each member of the Harvard graduating class wore only suits of homespun to commencement. A century later, in Utah, the wearing of homespun was for many a similar badge of honor. William Jennings, mayor of Salt Lake City in 1884, recalled:

One of the most important articles brought by

the pioneer women were [sic] their loom. For many years homespun woolen-linseys were all there was to wear. Brigham Young at one time decreed that men mustn't dance with any one in other than homespun garments; this was to discourage vanities and extravagances and to encourage home manufactures.[1]

The pride in self-sufficiency Brigham Young instilled in his followers was noted by Emma Caroll Seegmiller as she set down remembrances of her youth in the United Order of Orderville, Utah. In addition to the wearing of homespun, the shoes they wore in that community were handmade in their entirety: tanned in their own tannery with hide from their own cattle, and using tannery bark from their own trees.

> . . . topped off with our home-made straw hats, we became vividly distinctive, as self made-up as even President Brigham Young might have wished.[2]

Putting aside the criteria of piety, patriotism, and practicality, home manufactures placed a visual limitation on what even the most creative could accomplish with clothing and quilt. Plain or plaid, striped or checkered—these were the limited variations possible on the weaver's loom. Color was the only possible variation; Emma remembered

> . . . those large dye pots of indigo blue and aniline. The wild greasewood when steeped made a good yellow dye; when mixed with the indigo blue it made a very pretty green.[3]

But even young Emma, fervent young Daughter of Zion, could not resist factory-made fabrics:

> The figured calicoes in varied colors and designs . . . seemed so sheer compared with our usual homespun. And the "shiny" buttons, the neatly

folded papers of pins and cases of needles, the spools of thread, and best of all the "store smell" that went with it.[4]

It was this universal pleasure in the printed cloth, and the special excitement of store-bought, that linked her to the beginnings of the quiltmaker's craft. It bound her somehow across thousands of miles and almost one hundred years to the woman who pulled the treasures of another continent from her piece-bag.

The fabrics contained in this early small quilt (Figure 73) suggest that it covered one of America's privileged children. The fabric used for its backing is of whole cloth (the antislavery toile illustrated in Figure 69), and the center panel of the quilt's top is a substantial section of a red French toile, *Les Asphodel*. And that piece-bag yielded a large variety of other splendid fabrics. Several were large enough to form oversize triangles (including some additional bits of *Les*

FIGURE 73. *Whole-cloth center panel with one- and two-patch borders, circa 1800. Provenance unknown. 41" × 46". Cotton and linen. Collection of Robert B. Haas and Mariko Hibbett.*

Asphodel, suggesting the fabric had been used originally for a garment and its cutting-out left remnants of irregular shape). Still smaller pieces were cut into squares and even smaller triangles. This quiltmaker had access to the splendid fabric to which other women might only aspire.

CHAPTER
SEVEN

THE TOOLS

◆◆◆

WITH her piece-bag before her, or a strip of store-bought, the quiltmaker set to work. The tools she needed were small and few in number. In fact, they would fit into her apron pocket: scissors, needle and pins, thimble, and perhaps a handmade tape measure such as a marked ribbon. The tools might be splendid or simple, English or American;[1] but no matter what their description and origin, they were to be guarded, for easy replacement or replenishment was not always possible.

Needles and pins were particularly to be accounted for, and an ample supply of pins, even in the nineteenth century, suggested a certain economic status. As a discreet display of that status, one might work a Layette pincushion, another Small Endearment for a newborn. In these fashionable efforts, a message was spelled out in pins (most often manikin or dummy pins).

In her diary (December 30, 1771) Anna Green Winslow noted:

> My aunt stuck a white sattan pincushion for Mrs.
> Waters. On one side is a plathorn with flowers,

on the reverse, just under the border are on one side stuck these words, Josiah Waters, then follows on the end Decr. 1771, on the next side & end are the words Welcome little Stranger.[2]

Although these "sticking" pincushions marked other occasions and celebrations, that poignant phrase, "Welcome Little Stranger," may have been stuck more than any other, either alone or in variation. During the siege of Boston, a baby was given a pincushion that read "Welcome, little stranger, Though the port is closed"; and, in the early nineteenth century, another carried the message "God assist the mother through her danger, And protect the little stranger."[3]

Both the fundamental tools with which the quiltmaker worked and the basic elements of the quilt itself could be simple in line and number, or enhanced by all manner of extravagant adornment. The quilt could be plain or grand, worked for personal or political reasons, done in solitude or under the scrutiny of a circle of one's peers, but as a functional object it should serve to keep a body warm. Within the fundamental construction of the simple whole-cloth quilt is the essence of the quilt itself: a quilt top is separated from a backing by a batting or interlining, and all three components are then joined together with a small running stitch.

CHAPTER
EIGHT

THE CONSTRUCTION

✦✦✦

THE PIECED QUILT

THE technical challenge of the all-white quilt, or the subtle suggestion of social status in the use of the fine chintz for an elaborate appliqué temporarily defined these quilts as "best," a term used to imply an aristocracy among quilts. But the pieced quilts, simple or grand, emerged as the American quiltmaker's greatest glory.

Rigid social standards and a desire to keep pace with fashion abroad often caused the privileged classes to be less innovative. America's growing middle class often looked to those same standards, fearful of being considered gauche. Creative genius often results from the complete freedom that poverty allows.

The American pieced quilt was more the result of American circumstances than of European influences. Born of diverse requirements—warmth, thrift, beauty—its beginnings were directed in large part by women who had come from lower-middle-class or peasant stock, but the American quiltmaker, whatever her economic status, soon found herself increasingly drawn to its exciting visual possibilities.

Technique and pattern could be as finely worked by a woman of limited means as by the mistress of a Virginia plantation; available fabric was the only uncommon denominator.

Whatever her circumstances or abilities, the seemingly endless variations possible within a pieced pattern seemed to lead her to a disproportionate number of beginnings. The body of work a quiltmaker left to the next generation not only consisted of completed quilts, but usually included several tops that had never been quilted, or a stack of blocks that had never been formed into the whole, or single blocks worked to experiment with a particular pattern, or in some cases a sewing basket of small pieces never even worked into the beginning element. It is as though a sense of creative urgency pushed her to attempt a new pattern or to use a new bit of fabric before the work of her last inspiration had been brought to fruition. These other beginnings often worked their way into a quilt for a child—perhaps a sixth or seventh when there was less time for the sentimental preparations required for the arrival of a new baby.

Rather than the pastel slumber in which the twentieth century generally envelops its sleeping children, there was no special assignment of colors for the infants' quilts of the previous one hundred years. Nor does there seem to have been any special attempt to develop a repertoire of patterns specifically appropriate to the small subjects for which these

FIGURE 74. *Double Pyramids with four "H" corners and Sawtooth border, circa 1890. Lancaster County, Pennsylvania. 44" × 44". Cotton. Collection of Frank and Lucy Flanigan.* Courtesy of Edward Brown

FIGURE 75. *Fragmented blocks, circa 1890. Maine. 39¼" × 41½". Cotton. Collection of Pilgrim/Roy. A note found attached to the quilt reads "This is Grandpa R.'s cradle quilt. Aunt Lilla."*

quilts were made. In some instances the quiltmaker seems merely to have drawn from her sewing basket a block or two originally intended for another larger purpose and worked it, with other elements, into a quilt of smaller substance. The Double Pyramids (Figure 74) may in fact have had just such a casual beginning, as the fabrics in the center block do not appear elsewhere in the quilt, and the scale of that block required skillful handling to develop it into this original and innovative quilt. A Maine quilt of particular interest (Figure 75) contains a whole series of fragmented blocks. Several patterns are recognizable, but each block has been cut in half, as have been the sets. The center section of the quilt consists of three panels of these strange constructions—an unfinished quilt top, perhaps, cut and rearranged to make it seem less ponderous in the smaller area? Blocks of star patterns have also been cut and now form the quilt's borders. A note attached to the quilt reads "This is Grandpa R.'s cradle quilt. Aunt Lilla" but gives no clue to its creative origins.

Assembled elements were also worked into small summer spreads, although technically these are not quilts because of the absence of one or more of the elements essential to that definition. A summer spread, without backing or interlining, is distinct from a quilt top simply left unfinished by the presence of a concurrent binding of the outer edges and by the handling of the exposed seams of the quilt blocks themselves. In the case of appliqué blocks in a summer spread, after the blocks have been stitched to each other, the raw edges of the seams are turned inward toward each other and held together with a small running or a whipping stitch. This provides a finished look to the piece and prevents the cut edges from raveling. In pieced work, this system is impractical and the top is simply completed and then backed. No quilting is used, but occasionally the back is lightly tacked to the front in several spots to prevent its sagging.

The summer spread illustrated in Figure 77 was born of random beginnings. If a quiltmaker was of an orderly and fastidious nature, the small leftover scraps from another project might never find their way into a jumbled piece-bag, but would instead be promptly cut into tidy stacks of pre-determined shape and size for possible future projects: long,

FIGURE 76. *Summer Spread, circa 1840. Quiltmaker: Mrs. Sheldon. Brattleboro, Vermont. 51" × 51". Cottton. Private collection.* Courtesy of Steve Miller American Folk Art

FIGURE 77. *Two-patch with Saw-tooth border summer spread, circa 1880. Provenance unknown. 31" × 36". Cotton. Collection of Phyllis Haders.*

narrow strips for a Log Cabin quilt, or one-inch squares, or (if particularly small) triangles. As she found spare moments, the quiltmaker could reach into her basket and join light triangles to dark to form small squares later to be joined to each other, and then worked into blocks or strips or Sawtooth borders. In this small quilt, we can see that three distinct panels were sewn together, composed of 1,344 small triangles in all.

But most quilts were the result of the thoughtful arrangement of simple blocks, and it is in this aspect of the American quilt that we see the most extraordinary results of the quiltmaker's efforts. The viewer seems always to be immediately moved by a Star of Bethlehem or by a series of Mariner's Compasses worked across a small quilt, bedazzled by the mere presence of so many diamonds or narrow points—even when these diamonds or narrow points are badly sewn or unimaginatively set. It is in the consideration of the most simple of American pieced quilts that one can truly marvel at the quiltmaker's endless capacity for creating splendor from simplicity. Unlike appliqué, these compact units could be worked in the smallest of surroundings, held close to a lamp or fireplace in a crowded cabin, or worked in the lap as the great wagons crossed the prairies; they were born of whatever fabric was at hand.

As a young girl of four or five, the quiltmaker's first efforts were directed to an uneven four- or nine-patch block, and even when she had grown and her stitches became straight and true, she would return again and again to the simple shapes on which she had perfected the skills of her craft. She could work a simple pattern that had itself already been worked ten thousand times before in a like number of calico combinations and would introduce such sensitivity of scale and color and such innovations in borders and sets that the pattern was born new again.

Although a Diamond in a Square (Plate 62) shines most vividly in the large Amish quilts of Lancaster County, it also appears in multiple images on the smallest of pieced quilts. When the block is cut and stitched it can be set with others into simple sashing as in the Maine doll's quilt made by "Ida" for "Mary" (Figure 78). It can be embellished by the addition of multiple blocks of Broken Dishes (Figure 79); or diminished by setting the square not into another square but into narrow strips, then to be alternated with plain strips to form a Bars quilt (Plate 34). Or it can be worked of the finest

FIGURE 78. *Garden of Eden doll quilt, circa 1850. Quiltmaker: An inscription in ink on a back corner indicates it was made for "Ida" by "Mary" in Bremen, Maine. 13½" × 14½". Cotton. Collection of Betty Horton.*

FIGURE 79. *Broken Dishes variation, circa 1885. Pennsylvania. 34³/₄″ × 34³/₄″. Cotton. Collection of Kelter-Malcé Antiques.*

chintz to be set on point in diagonal strips using positive and negative images that will present the optical illusion of ever-emerging Variable Stars (Figure 80).

The simple four-patch can itself be turned into an elaborated Diamond in a Square and then worked into a delicate Lattice set (Figure 81); or be split into Pinwheels to be set apart with plain blocks (Figure 82)

This charmingly naive child's quilt (Figure 83) is technically classified as a two-block quilt. As with Irish Chain, for example, the overall design is dependent upon two separate geometric block designs being sewn alternately to one another across the quilt's top. In this case, the four-patch was elaborated for the first block, then elaborated once again by dividing each of the original pieces into diagonal halves.

The nine-patch block, because of its geometric configuration, was divided into multiple variations of patterns. The simple squares were cut apart and rearranged and cut apart again. But in the most original of children's quilts, we find the piece is based not on the multiple variations at the quiltmaker's command, but on the nine-patch in its purest and most fundamental form. Although borders and set may

FIGURE 80. *Variable Star illusion with chintz border, circa 1825. New York State. 32" × 43". Collection of Linda and Irwin Berman.*

FIGURE 81. *Four-patch variation in diagonal Lattice set, circa 1840. New England. 41" × 41". Cotton. Collection of Linda and Irwin Berman.*

FIGURE 82. *Pinwheel with multiple borders, circa 1845. Pennsylvania. 37" × 37". Cotton. Private collection.* Photograph courtesy of America Hurrah Antiques

FIGURE 83. *Four-patch variation, circa 1850. Provenance unknown. 28½" × 34¾". Cotton. Collection of the author.*

be given great attention, the heart of the quilt is a block composed of nine simple cotton squares. It is perhaps a sentimental link to the quilt she had first worked years ago for her rag-baby; the love and attention she lavished upon her doll child transferred to a sweet babe of her own.

BORDERS

The elegant Hexagon quilt illustrated in Plate 8 surely came from the hands of a woman in sophisticated surroundings. The hexagons themselves offer an abundance of beautiful floral chintzes, many of them retaining their original glaze. The border surrounding this richness of remnants is itself a fine, roller-printed chintz. In order to perfectly continue the stripe around the entire quilt, its maker mitered each of the four corners—not unexpectedly, considering the perfection of all of the other elements.

Although one might see a mitered corner on the borders of a small appliqué quilt (perhaps meant to hold a running-vine border), in American quilts both large and small, even when the quiltmaker was concerned with demonstrating her skill, the great majority of whole-cloth borders are constructed in much simpler fashion. Two strips are added on alternate sides, and to those extended surfaces the final two strips are sewn. The odd strips of chintz were often used on the smallest of quilts—and in the quilts in Plates 9 and 10 two separate chintz fabrics have been put to use in the border areas of each.

A border of particular delicacy was worked on the very edge of the *broderie perse* in Plate 3. It was this type of border that was often found on the large *broderie perse* quilts that were the aesthetic inspirations for such smaller pieces. A strip of fabric was attached to the outer edge of the quilt, cut, turned into points, and finely appliquéd to the quilt's

FIGURE 85. *Nine-patch with Toad in the Puddle variation corner blocks, circa 1845. New York. 28″ × 34″. Wool challis. Private collection.* Photograph courtesy of America Hurrah Antiques

FIGURE 86. *Exaggerated nine-patch with Zigzag border, circa 1880. Provenance unknown. 33½" × 39½". Cotton. Collection of Jim and Sandy Stephenson*. Courtesy of Stella Rubin

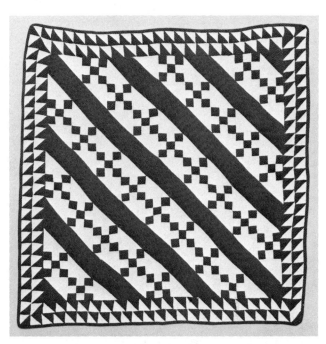

FIGURE 87. *Nine-patch with diagonal Bars and Double Sawtooth border, circa 1865. Ohio. 34¼" × 34¼". Cotton. Collection of Stella Rubin.*

surface. The popularity of this border (also echoed in quilted form on the all-white quilt in Plate 5) declined in the second quarter of the century but continued in pieced form, especially in inner borders. On the earlier quilts, the appliquéd border was called by its English name, Dog's Tooth, but the later pieced variation was more often referred to as Pyramids.

The use of a multiple border around a central design was adapted to the small quilts from the larger center-medallion quilts of English origin that greatly influenced the American quilts of the late eighteenth and early nineteenth century. In Figure 18, the scale and placement of each element within the borders has been appropriately resolved.

Multiple strips of solid fabric were also added to the main body of American quilts. In many instances, each would receive a separate quilting pattern, and extravagant appliqué borders were worked when appropriate, but it was in her choice and design of the pieced borders that the quiltmaker could often bring to her work the greatest sense of individuality.

Flying Geese, in border as well as block, was a staple on American quilts. A quiltmaker on the Kees Homestead in New York State may have looked with faint dissatisfaction

FIGURE 88. *Winged Square with Zigzag border, circa 1890. Mennonite. Lehigh County, Pennsylvania. 40" × 60". Cotton. Collection of M. Finkel and Daughter.*

at her relatively sedate set of Rose Wreath blocks, and in a burst of effort added multiple borders of oversize Flying Geese (Plate 14).

No other border was applied with greater ingenuity and diversity than the Sawtooth. It could be applied in one of three methods to a perfect turn and direction, but it is in its less precise applications that it often assumed its greatest charm. In some instances the border threatens to overwhelm the area it was merely meant to contain (Figure 89). The quiltmaker more caught up with exuberance than with excellence would simply work the required lengths, and cut and attach them as needed. The discerning quiltmaker was

more cautious and saw to it that the proportions and length fit the piece to be bordered—such was obviously not the concern of the quiltmaker who worked the Variable Star medallion in Figure 90.

BACKING AND BATTING

Once the top had been cut (if of whole cloth) or constructed (should the quiltmaker choose another of the variety of techniques available to her), the backing itself would likewise be cut or constructed. Although of secondary visual consideration, the backing of a quilt can hold unexpected aesthetic delights, and it may be rich with additional clues as to the date and provenance of the quilt and the economic status of the quiltmaker.

The use of a splendid piece of toile or chintz as a backing is, on a large quilt, generally a reliable indication that the piece was worked in an atmosphere of economic means and accessibility. The reverse of Figure 100 is a backing of an early block print of oak leaves and acorns, an extravagant use of the printed cloth that was so dearly bought. On these smaller pieces, the necessary amount, and therefore the cost, was of smaller consideration; but the consideration was still too great for a woman of moderate means.

The most popular backing was the most practical—a piece of white cloth, usually, in the early decades of the nineteenth century, of homespun linen. Even on the small back surface of a child's quilt, it might be pieced rather than whole, salvaged perhaps from pieces of household linens or a small area separated from sections worn beyond hope of repair. While linen was difficult to dye, later imported or domestic cotton or cotton homespun were more easily enhanced with natural or commercial dyes. The back of the Amish quilt in Figure 59, for example, is a coarse homespun dyed with walnut or butternut hulls. It is more likely that the backing itself was cut from another, already dyed piece of cloth rather than dyed specifically for this purpose.

A backing might bear faint markings to remind us of its beginnings as a utilitarian bag for flour or feed. The exaggerated nine-patch in Figure 86 is backed with finer goods,

but its advertising stamp also remains. Although the image has been turned inward toward the cotton batting and we must read it in reverse, we see the figure of a woman seated at a sewing machine and within the double circle that surrounds her we read the assurance of a "PURE SOFT FINISH FOR MACHINE AND HAND SEWING."

When store-bought calicoes grew in abundance, they were, of course, used more often as a backing for children's quilts. Even then they were often faded from previous use. It is not unusual to turn back a section of a Pennsylvania quilt of any size, however, to discover the backing composed of gawdy strips of store-bought calico, new from the bolts.

In addition to leftover strips and remnants of substantial size, backings often proved to be a thrifty repository for an assortment of odd scraps and leftover pieced blocks. In most instances, design and workmanship clearly define the top of the quilt from the backing, but it is not unusual to find the reverse of the quilt of more interest. The backing of an ordinary four-patch child's quilt (Figure 91) is composed of an economical arrangement of the quiltmaker's miscellaneous leavings: odd-shaped strips of fabric holding together two blocks of Diamond in a Square, an exaggerated nine-

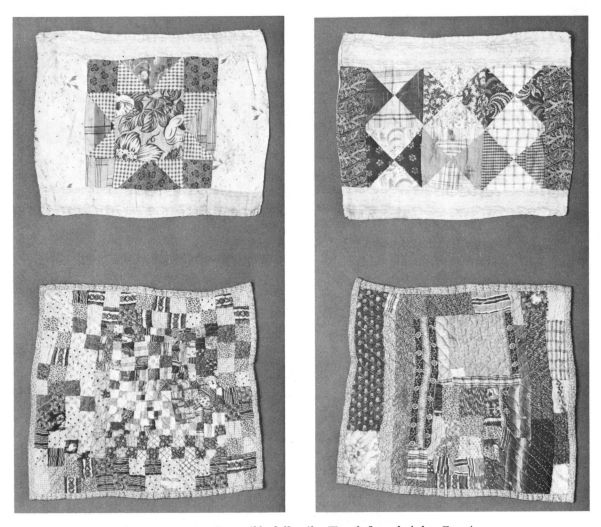

FIGURES 92 AND 93. *Reversible doll quilts.* Top left and right: *Evening Star (front) and Broken Dishes (back), circa 1825. Pennsylvania. 9½" × 12½". Cotton. Collection of Stella Rubin. Bottom left and right: Four-patch expanding (front) and Crazy Quilt (back), circa 1875. Quiltmaker: Marie Landis. Boiling Springs, Pennsylvania. 11" × 12". Cotton. Collection of Evie Gleason.*

patch, and a section of Rocky Glen. One of the two small doll's quilts illustrated in Figures 92 and 93 neatly makes use of leftover pieced work on its front and back. The other has constructed "new" cloth from such tiny bits of cotton they were surely drawn from the deepest corners of an almost empty piece-bag.

PLATE 50. *Log Cabin center block with diagonal striped inner border, circa 1895. Amish. Tuscawaras County, Ohio. 38" × 39". Wool. Collection of Darwin D. Bearley.*

PLATE 51. *Diamonds, circa 1885. Amish. Holmes County, Ohio. 31" × 37". Cotton. Collection of Darwin D. Bearley.*

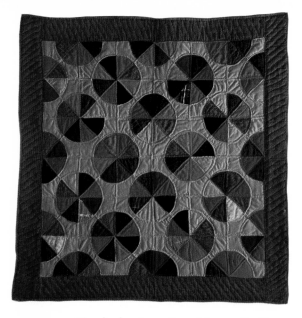

PLATE 57. *Pinwheels, circa 1890. Mennonite. Pennsylvania. 36½" × 37". Cotton. Private collection.* Photograph courtesy of America Hurrah Antiques

PLATE 58. *Log Cabin with striped border, circa 1895. Amish, Geauga County, Ohio. 29" × 31½". Wool and cotton. Collection of Darwin D. Bearley.*

PLATE 59. *Log Cabin, Barn Raising variation with diagonal-stripe border, circa 1875. Lancaster County, Pennsylvania. 36¾" × 37½". Cotton and wool. Collection of Marilyn and Ron Kowaleski.*

PLATE 60. *Log Cabin variation, circa 1865. Amish. Lancaster County, Pennsylvania. 42" × 43½". Wool. Collection of Carl and Elizabeth Safanda.*

PLATE 61. *Railroad Crossing, circa 1895. Amish. Medina County, Ohio. 37" × 51". Cotton. Collection of Frank and Lucy Flanigan.* Courtesy of Kiracofe and Kile

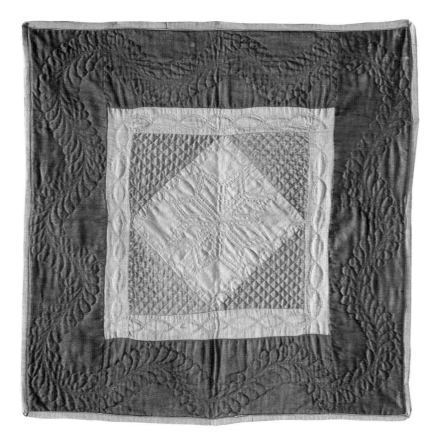

PLATE 62. *Diamond in a Square, circa 1890. Amish. Lancaster County, Pennsylvania. 40" × 40". Wool. Collection of America Hurrah Antiques.*

PLATE 66. *Log Cabin, Straight Furrow variation cradle quilt, 1980. Quiltmaker: Sandi Fox. Los Angeles, California. 23¼″ × 27¾″. Cotton. Collection of Mr. and Mrs. Franklin W. Knowlton.*

PLATE 67. *Pineapple, 1980. Quiltmaker: Sandi Fox. Los Angeles, California. 40″ × 40″. Cotton. Collection of Marsha and Ed Bronsky.*

PLATE 68. *Roman Stripes, 1981. Quiltmaker: Sandi Fox. Los Angeles, California. 32″ × 32″. Cotton. Collection of the quiltmaker.*

PLATE 69. *Diamond in the Square with multiple borders, 1983. Quiltmaker: Sandi Fox. Los Angeles, California. 35¹/2" × 35¹/2". Cotton. Collection of the quiltmaker.*

PLATE 70. *Tumbling Blocks, 1982. Quiltmaker: Sandi Fox. Los Angeles, California. 28¹/4" × 36¹/2". Cotton. Collection of the quiltmaker.*

PLATE 71. *T's with Sawtooth and LeMoyne Star borders, 1980. Quiltmaker: Sandi Fox. Los Angeles, California. 40" × 40". Cotton. Private collection.*

There are children's quilts—although few in number—that were painstakingly designed and worked to be truly reversible. One could not hope to find a better example than the Walk Around and Variable Star and nine-patch illustrated in Plates 23 and 24. Each in itself forms a perfect top, and they join to form a perfect and truly reversible quilt. The placement of the double inscription noting the name and date of birth of Master Alfred P. Sawyer (Figure 94) is our only indication of the intended top.

When the back of the small quilt had been prepared, it would be placed face down, ready for the batting, which was made of the same materials found in full-size quilts. Washed and carded wool or cotton were the interlinings used in the great majority of American quilts. Eighteenth- and early nineteenth-century quilts more often reflected the wider availability of wool, but cotton, when available, became the batting of choice.

Later in the century, one was apt to find an interlining of soft flannel, or a piece of loosely woven wool that had finished serving its original purpose. These were particularly appropriate for pressed quilts (Log Cabin and Crazy Quilts) and for the intricate flat surfaces worked by the Amish.

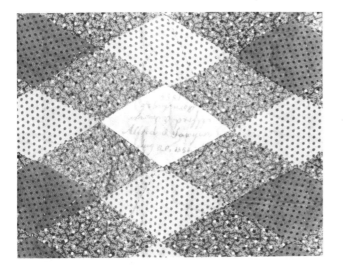

FIGURE 94. *Walk Around (detail), 1856 (dated). See Plate 23. Lowell, Massachusetts. 50" × 50". Cotton. Collection of George Kiberd and May Tow.*

Commercial cotton batting was in use by the middle of the century, but many rural children continued to retrieve precious wool caught on fences and bushes. Similar gatherings occurred as families moved out West: many children retrieved bits of buffalo fur that clung to scrub and desert weeds as they walked beside their parents on route to the Great Salt Lake Valley.

QUILTING

The finished top, on which the quiltmaker's creative efforts had to that point been focused, was carefully spread over the batting or interlining. Basting stitches were worked to hold backing, batting, and top together in preparation for quilting, a critical element in both function and design. To a previously flat surface, the quilting stitches added the dimensional subtleties of light and shadow. The selected quilting pattern was a linear element inscribed in thread to echo or counterpoint those lines already defined by seam and color.

Except for the occasional instance in which a particular tension was required (as in the case of stuffed work), it is probable that most of these small quilts were not set into a frame to be quilted. Even when the piece was full size, a woman often chose to hold the carefully basted layers in her lap to be quilted, or to work on a table top. It was then easier to pick up at odd moments and less demanding of space.

The quilting frame was used for large quilts either by women who preferred it or during a quilting bee; but the quilting bee is both reality and myth. Women *did* gather at festive intervals around a quilting frame (in many instances no more than four boards between a like number of chairs) to participate in an activity usually of greater social than creative significance. The top that waited to be quilted by a group of willing hands—often, alas, of uneven ability— provided a reason for a gathering among women often physically isolated from each other. If simple companionship was not enough, a more defined purpose would be established for a quilting bee by the working of a quilt to mark a rite of passage in the life of a son or daughter now too big for the small quilt that covered his or her childhood bed. One of the legal traditions brought from England to her

FIGURE 95. *Nine-patch variation with inner Pyramid border, circa 1880. Lancaster County, Pennsylvania. 24″ × 30″. Cotton. Collection of Bettie Mintz, 'All of Us Americans' Folk Art.*

American colonies was the mark of independence accorded a young man on his twenty-first birthday. In this country, it became a tradition not of law but of affection for female relatives and acquaintances to honor a young man on that important occasion by presenting him with a Freedom Quilt. Friends might gather to celebrate a young lady's engagement by quilting the dozen tops she had constructed since she was a child, tops stored unquilted in many instances to postpone the expense of batting and backing until a betrothal was imminent. These quilting bees were confirmation by a small community of family and friends of the importance of life's common experiences. They were a feminine expression of dependency on one's neighbors even in an age of fierce independence, a softer side to the American spirit.

Young girls stood beside their mothers, threading needles, seeing their own future in the tableaux before them. The role she would assume when she was old enough, and skilled enough, to take her place in that special circle was the role society had assigned to her, and it was the role in which she gladly envisioned her grown-up self.

But as with most intensely creative endeavors, the majority of masterpiece quilts, and those with the most tender inspiration, surely were worked in solitude. So much of the guiltmaker was worked into those Small Endearments— would she not have wished the message it held to be written by her hand alone?

The quilting pattern chosen for each small quilt was marked on the waiting top in a number of ways. The woman who used a pencil truly believing it would wash out was no doubt distraught to find it never really did. Sometimes a chalked thread was held taut and flicked to deposit chalk dust in a straight line; but this, or methods such as pouncing a bit of cinnamon onto the cloth through a perforated paper, left an indistinct line, open to smudging and difficult to remove. A line marked with a piece of chalk or a sliver of soap was too wide to follow accurately the intended design. The master quilter would use the blunt point of a tapestry needle and, holding it at an angle parallel to the cloth, would mark or crease the cloth along the side of a ruler or around a template of more intricate design. (She might also press in a pattern from a metal or wooden template utensil similar to a cookie cutter.) Placing the work on a hard surface to mark each section as needed, the layers of her quilt would hold the indentations until the quiltmaker replaced them with the small, even stitches that were her special challenge.

The thread she used was almost always white. A colored thread was difficult to make colorfast and often left a deposit on the cloth as it was pulled through. The availability of white thread, a staple of her household and, in the early decades, generally of home manufacture, was also a factor in its use. But of equal importance was the visibility of the stitch to be worked, for that stitch and the design in which it appeared were the standards by which she was judged. One will occasionally see a bit of colored thread used in the latter half of the century, either in contrast or in compatibility, but stitches of green thread on green calico would not accomplish the delicate overlay of pattern that was the quiltmaker's usual intent.

The needle—long or "between," straight or slightly curved, according to personal preference—was threaded with a length usually less than eighteen inches. A longer piece of thread would be weakened as the thread nearest the needle's eye was continually pulled through the fabrics and batting. A firm knot was tied or rolled onto the end of the thread, and as the needle was initially pulled from back to front, a sharp tug would pull the knot through the backing to lodge itself in the batting. At the end of a line of stitches, or a length of thread, another knot would be formed just above the cloth. The needle was then reinserted in the last exit hole and run under the backing and through the batting one or two inches, parallel to the quilt. Another sharp tug would pull that knot through. The cloth was then gathered on the remaining length of thread, and when the thread was snipped, the reflattened cloth would cover the cut tail. The back of the quilt should show no beginnings or endings, but the life of the quilt itself was dependent on both being there, firm and fixed.

It was important to make the stitches both even and small. Bracing the eye of the needle against her thimble, the quiltmaker would put two to six stitches on the needle before pulling it through. It was the conscientious quiltmaker's goal to work at least twenty stitches to the inch (ten on the top and ten on the bottom), all perfectly straight and evenly spaced.

The running stitch itself, as with other techniques and designs in all areas of American craftsmanship, was an adaptation designed to meet the needs of an emerging nation. The English quilter preferred a backstitch, but a running stitch took less time and used less thread, both precious commodities. Although the backstitch is perceived to be a stronger stitch, the running stitch used by the American quilter was more pliable, more capable of responding to the quilt's movement without breaking.

In the early part of the nineteenth century, the quilting itself—often to a greater degree than the design of the quilt top—was the creative and technical measure by which the quiltmaker was judged, and it is unusual to find a nineteenth-century child's quilt that was quilted on the sewing machine. Even when the machines were available and in use for common household production, women still used their hands to establish their creative reputation. Piecing of a utilitarian nature might be done on the machine by someone not inclined to use her quilts as an avenue for personal excellence or expression—late in the century the Amish quiltmaker relied heavily on her foot-driven machine to sew together the great large pieces of cloth that formed the surface for her magnificent hand quilting—but it was generally understood that the best quilts were those in which the human hand translated into reality the mind's design and the heart's desire. Yet we find a carefully worked Cherry Wreath (Plate 43) with some elements of the top and the entire intricate quilting pattern done by machine. This fine quilt might have been an ambitious exercise by a woman eager to show off a symbol of her affluence, and as such might have been worked on one of the first sewing machines to be installed in a Mechanicsburg, Pennsylvania, parlor.

The aesthetic sensibilities of the quiltmaker alerted her to the fact that the scale of her small pieced and appliquéd statements did not often lend themselves to the elaborate plumes and feathered wreaths that she used with such enthusiasm in the embellishment of her larger works. Such motifs do, of course, appear—as on the plain blocks separating the Sawtooth Stars in Figure 10—but they are more the occasional instance.

Even when the figurative motifs proved either impractical

or impossible, there remained a rich tradition of geometric patterns upon which she could draw, and these small quilts are an amazing repository for their multiple variations. A whole-cloth quilt was usually quilted in an all-over pattern, tiny stitches in shapes and arrangement not unique to the American quilt but drawn from the same instinctive filling of space we find in the art and craft of other cultures. On occasion we find an entire pieced quilt bearing the same all-over quilting (Figure 83 is worked with bands of Ocean Wave or Shell quilting), but the use of the filling patterns was generally reserved for specific areas within the quilt and was coupled with other quilted motifs or patterns.

The quilting patterns that overlay the strong geometric pieces contained in the Amish quilt in Figure 59 are in themselves another pattern. A central area of Diamond or Cross-Hatching expands outward into additional borders composed not of fabric but of distinctive and complimentary areas of tiny quilted stitches. The lines of the quilting pattern

FIGURE 96. *Variable Star, circa 1885. Amish. Ohio. 34½″ × 41½″. Cotton. Collection of Sandra Mitchell.*

are in fact more intricate and diverse than the simple squares and rectangles over which they are worked.

In viewing a group of nineteenth-century quilts, the eye will always be drawn to, and find immediate pleasure in, a glazed chintz border or a bit of stuffed work. Occasionally, however, an otherwise ordinary quilt will exhibit extraordinary distinction in its quilting, and the observer would do well not to overlook even those that appear most simple. It is just such a quilt that covered Mrs. Wickersham's infant daughter. The common brown fabric used in its Checkerboard blocks is faded; the quilt itself has long been separated from family and affection, but the traces of its shining beginnings are still there. Simple of line, it is a carefully wrought sampler of quilting patterns and motifs. The center blocks hold the outlines of two types of flowers and a geometric leaf pattern quilted into the small brown squares, and in its small external triangles are tiny sunbursts and leafy branches. Still the quilter was not done! In the four corner patches are tulips and in the four corners the smallest of quilted hearts. The four outside blocks are quilted simply, by-the-piece (that is, following the outline of the pieces of fabric), and the remaining four blocks record four basic all-over filling patterns: Cross-Hatch, Clamshell, Chevron, and Tea Cup. And there, in her final stitches, the quiltmaker has entered in tiny red cross-stitches the dear child's name: Sarah Emma Wickersham, 1847 (see detail, Figure 97).

The most splendid of quilted lines were reserved for the elaborate all-white quilts that a nineteenth-century needlewoman often considered to be her crowning achievement. Especially during the first third of the century, the classical purity of a white surface was much admired in all decorative arts, and this neoclassical influence is apparent on the more formally designed all-white quilts through the use of a center medallion surrounded by geometric forms. But the figurative expression of natural forms also found its way into more romantically arranged surfaces—small quilts resplendent with plumes and ribbons, lush grapes and leaves. The most exceptional of these all-white children's quilts were worked well before the middle of the century. They were both made and treasured beyond that date but, as with all work of the hands, there was a perceptible decline both in quantity and quality.

FIGURE 97. *Checkerboard (detail), 1847 (dated). Provenance unknown. 36" × 36". Cotton. Private collection.* Courtesy of Kiracofe and Kile

Beyond the linear intricacies of their designs, the remarkable aspect of these quilts is the heightened dimensional quality of the surface, achieved through the careful stuffing of additional cotton batting, and in some instances cording, into certain areas of the quilted design. This could be accomplished through the use of any one of three techniques:

1. The construction and components of the all-white quilt were identical to that of the whole-cloth quilt, with two exceptions: top and back were of course pure white, and the technique generally required that a slightly more loosely woven cloth be used for the backing. Once the three layers had been basted, the desired pattern was quilted across the entire top. The piece was then turned to the back, and in the middle of each area or motif to be especially emphasized, threads were very carefully separated (*never* cut, except by the most casual quilter) and bits of cotton or cording were carefully inserted until the desired density and elevation had been achieved. The threads were then realigned, and if the weave remained somewhat distorted, with the first washing it would return to the straight.

2. Particularly where the stuffed elements were small and intricate, or where the quiltmaker did not wish other than a cloth of excellent quality and weave as the back of her quilt, the top fabric was simply basted

FIGURE 98. *All-white quilt, circa 1840. Southwestern Ohio. 43" × 45" including fringe. Cotton. Collection of Janis Ito.* Courtesy of Kiracofe and Kile

to an extremely loosely woven piece of gauzelike fabric. Only the areas to be stuffed were then quilted in outline and they were stuffed quite easily from the back through the open-weave cloth. These isolated sections completed, a regular cotton batting or interlining and a regular white backing would be added. Additional quilting would then be worked around the prestuffed areas, and background or filling quilting would be worked throughout the quilt. These first two techniques can be differentiated, even in a finished piece, by inspecting the reverse of the quilt. In the first instance, the quilting pattern on the front is identical to that on the back. In the other, only those lines worked after the initial stuffing will be visible on the reverse.

3. The third possibility, used to perfection in the quilt illustrated in Plate 5 (also see detail in Figure 4), is known as Marseilles quilting. Since a complete batting or interlining is not held between the two layers, it is not, by rigid definition, a quilt. It was considered as such, however, and is important to a study of the early development of the all-white quilt. Again, a fine but often more loosely woven cloth is used for the backing, but in this case it is basted directly to the

plain white top. Once again, the complete quilting pattern is worked across the quilt, and cotton batting or cording, or a combination of both, is carefully inserted in specific areas through the backing, again through separated threads. The areas left unstuffed may have no quilting pattern (none is required because there is no batting to be held in place) but may also be intricately quilted in fine but flat designs. The absence of batting throughout the quilt makes the use of this technique easily identifiable.

Perhaps it is the extraordinary refinement and sophistication of these pieces that prevents one from calling them what they are: stuffed work. Too many contemporary observers seem perversely intent upon using the term "trapunto," a twentieth-century word describing a style of eighteenth-century needlework. It is an inaccurate and inappropriate label for this technique, because it was neither known to, nor used by, the women whose work we celebrate here.

BINDING

Once the quilting was completed, the batting and (unless it was to be used as a part of the binding) the backing were carefully trimmed even with the quilt top. The manner in which the raw edges were then covered was a matter of individual creative choice, and all of the final niceties of adult quilts are found on those for children and dolls.

On occasion, front and back were simply folded in toward each other and the edge then held closed with small whipping stiches. On a reversible quilt such as the whole-cloth quilt in Figure 100, the use of this technique was no doubt based on aesthetic criteria, but the disadvantage of this method was the lack of protection it afforded the quilt's edges, those parts most apt to show wear.

On other quilts, only the batting was trimmed away and the backing was then brought to the front and sewn down. It was the mark of a good needleworker that this be no more than one-quarter of an inch.

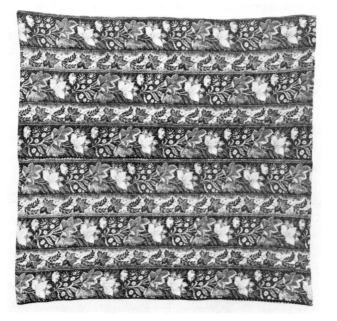

FIGURE 100. *Whole-cloth quilt, circa 1825. Provenance unknown. 42" × 45¾". Cotton. The back of the quilt is a roller-printed design of acorns and oak leaves. Collection of Bettie Mintz, 'All of Us Americans' Folk Art.*

Both of these methods could accommodate a bright bit of cotton piping. In the first instance, it was simply inserted between the turned-under edges of the front and back before they were sewn together; and, in the second, it was inserted between the folded-over backing and the quilt top, as in Plate 18. The use of piping was not common, and is most often observed on quilts circa 1835–1865, particularly those made in the Western Reserve.

The binding most commonly found on a nineteenth-century quilt, large or small, is a separate binding, generally constructed from a one-inch strip of fabric. Placed face down on the quilt's top, it was sewn in place with a fine running stitch, brought to the back, a quarter-inch turned under, and the binding on the reverse then slip-stitched into place. This left one-quarter inch visible front and back, allowing the quiltmaker to complete her work with a small bit of contrasting fabric, if that was her choice. Because commercial binding, particularly in the twentieth century, was cut on the bias, it is often incorrectly assumed to have been the norm in the previous century. On most nineteenth-century quilts, however, where a separate binding was used, it was cut on the straight of the goods. This represented a more economical use of the fabric and could allow the binding to further embellish the border with yet another element of design—a striped fabric, for example, or a bright row of tiny dots or circles. From a purely practical point of view, should eventually wear on the binding necessitate its replacement, this is the only one of the three basic binding methods that would alow the binding to be removed and replaced leaving the original top, back, and quilting stitches intact.

These techniques were used on children's quilts throughout the nineteenth century. They provided the functional protection of the quilt edges, but in design allowed only the most simple addition of color and contrast. Bindings on the quilts made in the earliest part of the century, however, exhibited a refinement and attention to detail that were generally apparent in every aspect of pre-1850 pieces.

English Jacobean embroidery was characterized by a rigid formality and by heavily worked backgrounds. The relaxed lines and open spaces on this piece of American crewelwork (Figure 101) are typical of the transitional changes in tech-

FIGURE 101. *Embroidered urn and flowers, circa 1800. Provenance unknown. 32⅛" × 41⅝". Cotton, wool, and linen. Collection of The Henry Francis du Pont Winterthur Museum.*

nique and design as needleworkers moved from Old World to New. This child's quilt is a cotton twill, woven in a diamond pattern and quilted with diagonal running stitches. Embroidered with Romanian couching, outline, cross-, and chainstitches in blue, brown, and beige, it may in fact have been cut down from a larger and earlier piece, perhaps worked in the eighteenth century. The narrow tape binding indicates, however, that even if reworked, by the first quarter of the nineteenth century, it was intended to cover a smaller soul.

In both eighteenth and early nineteenth centuries, the tape (or braid) that bound the quiltmaker's splendid quilts was also in more common use around her home. it was used to tie her dress or her bonnet, or to pull closed her sewing pocket. Although this type of tape was commercially im-

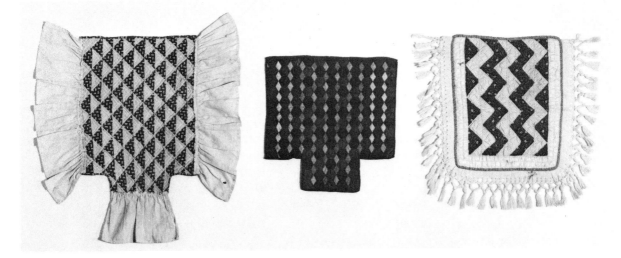

FIGURE 102. Left: *Birds-in-the-Air doll quilt, circa 1830. Maine. 21" × 20¼", including a 4¾" ruffle added by sewing machine sometime after 1860. Cotton. Collection of Kiracofe and Kile.* Middle: *Honeycomb doll quilt, circa 1825. Provenance unknown. 13¼" × 13½". Silk and cotton. Collection of Kiracofe and Kile.* Right: *Streak of Lightning doll quilt, circa 1840. Pennsylvania. 19" × 17¼". Cotton. Collection of Kiracofe and Kile. The border fabric retains a slight glaze and supports a 3½" handmade cotton fringe.*

ported, for the most part it was handwoven, either on a hand or box loom. It was considered fashionable pick-up work, but was such fundamental weaving that its production could be undertaken even by a young girl.

The dust ruffle later added to the Maine four-poster doll quilt (Figure 102) is a reminder of certain larger quilts from the eighteenth and nineteenth centuries. The fringe on the small Streak of Lightning was an ambitious adornment that found its way onto a number of first- and second-quarter quilts for children of the privileged class, either woven (Figures 98 and 99, Plates 5 and 7) or netted (Plate 4).

INSCRIPTIONS

Either with her final stitches, or in the course of the quilt top's construction, the quiltmaker would often add a name and date to document the intent of the creative effort. The inscription of names and initials was an American preoccupation: on ornate calling cards left in Victorian parlors, or carved into Independence Rock by the pioneers on their move westward.

By mid-century, it had become popular practice for members of a group to affix their signatures to a special quilt. It might be for the purpose of raising funds for the Methodist Church or for the Women's Christian Temperance Union; but more often the inscription was an affirmation of friendship and affection. This child's quilt (Figure 103) would surely have welcomed a small new member to the Massachusetts community in which it was made. Red and white quilts containing elements of embroidery (often figures of children and animals worked in red cotton floss) were popular during the latter part of the century. This quilt contains pieced, appliquéd, and embroidered blocks, most with a decidedly nautical theme. Small red and white pieced triangles form the Feathered Star signed by L. T. and F. U. Norton and are elongated to represent the Rising Sun on which the names of Mr. and Mrs. Thomas H. Verge are recorded. Mr.

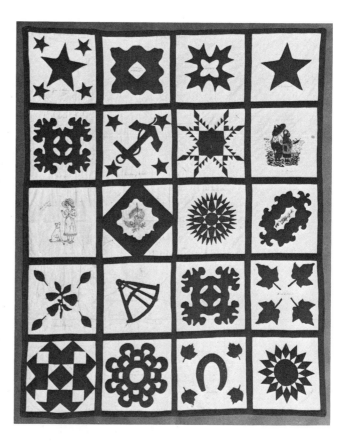

FIGURE 103. *Album Quilt with nautical theme, 1883 (dated). Massachusetts. 50½″ × 63″. Cotton. Collection of Kelter-Malcé Antiques.*

FIGURE 104. *Birds-in-the-Air variation doll quilt (detail), 1851 (dated). Philadelphia, Pennsylvania. 16¾″ × 16¾″. Cotton. Collection of Smith and Wanda Johnson.*

FIGURE 105. *John M. Lyon Centennial quilt, 1876 (dated). New York State. 41½″ × 41½″. Cotton. Collection of Linda and Irwin Berman.*

and Mrs. J. R. Dellow contributed an appliquéd Anchor and Stars and the Sextant signed by Wm. Griffin was imaginatively worked on a sewing machine. The Noyes (Fannie L., Georgie L., and Harry K.) joined Isa J. Russell in signing the block containing an embroidered eagle and standard. Horace M. and Anna D. Sargent signed their names above an embroidered girl and dog and then thoughtfully added the date, 1883, to provide us with the year of the quilt's presentation. The most intriguing block on the quilt is surely the one signed by Eugene L. Ramsdell. In a variety of red floss, worked in fine cross-stitch, a boy and girl stand with their backs to us looking out to sea to view a sinking ship. Underneath this scene is written in ink, "What are the wild waves saying, Sister?" The lucky child for whom this quilt was worked must have been surrounded by a number of family members and friends, as thirty-five names appear on the twenty blocks in a variety of script.

On occasion, the inscription is one of subtle suggestion—initials and date worked on a piece of linen and appliquéd to a simple doll's quilt to add both identification and distinction (Figure 104). On another, we might find an extravagant arrangement of information, such as on the splendid quilt worked for Master John M. Lyon (Figure 105).

On most quilts, however, their origin and destination is unmarked, a secret still held. These small quilts (Figures 106 and 107) might have been worked for twins, but they were separated long ago. Their images are joined here to tell a story we cannot read, sister quilts together again.

FIGURE 106. *Sunburst with Variable Star and Birds-in-the-Air border, circa 1850. Lehigh County, Pennsylvania. 37″ × 39″. Cotton. Collection of Rosemarie and Richard Machmer.*

FIGURE 107. *Sunburst with Birds-in-the-Air border, circa 1850. Lehigh County, Pennsylvania. 41″ × 41″. Cotton. Collection of Linda and Irwin Berman.*

Epilogue

◆◆◆

THE bitter truths of infant mortality were carved in stone up and down the Eastern Seacoast and scratched on boards and boulders across the wild prairie, and they were understood by the smallest observers. With resignation and acceptance, the fact that life was brief and eternity long was duly noted on the phrases young girls, under the supervision of their elders, worked on their childhood samplers. A child of seven had marked in threads:

> *And now my soul another year*
> *Of thy short life is past*
> *I cannot long continue here*
> *And this may be my last*

On an English sampler of 1776, Ann French entered

> *The work in hand my friends may have*
> *When I am dead and in my grav* (sic)

and variations of this phrase were echoed on hundreds of other pieces, among them Sarah Briton's, done in America in 1806:

The work in hand my friends may have
When I am in the silent grave

As late as 1839 Margaret Morgan, within a border of honeysuckle, pansies, and rosebuds still acknowledged

There is an hour when I must die
Nor can I tell how soon twill come
A thousand children young as I
Are called by death to hear their doom.

The same cross-stitches and alphabetical configurations that formed these pessimistic pronouncements also marked names and dates on nineteenth-century quilts for children, but it was then in an unspoken statement of optimism rather than of resignation. When they were entered on those Small Endearments, the acceptance of mortality expressed on the samplers was replaced with an affirmation of faith, faith even in the face of the infant death that touched almost every American family.

Children continued to die, but in the end it was not the cholera or the typhoid that diminished the glory of those early quilts for America's children. Those evils came quietly. It was the Industrial Revolution, all machinery and noise, that took away the creative confidence that had resulted in a century of individual expression.

Quilts continued to be made, of course, and with the same affection—but with a different delight. The pure pleasure visible in the discovery and the development of the craft was replaced with iron-on transfers and the printed pattern. The quiltmaker who had so brilliantly translated into textiles the reality and refinement of self and country now became reliant on another's interpretation. She continued to sing the song, but another now wrote the words.

It is the very qualities we celebrate in the craft's beginnings that contemporary quiltmakers too often ignore. The qualities of individual expression were set down with a pride in craftsmanship. These Small Endearments were made not just to cover and delight that one small child, but to carry a portion of the quiltmaker's best self to another generation, and to a generation and another beyond that. Pride in the work of her hands was often noted with a craftsman's mark, the outline of her hand worked in small quilted stitches.

But other hands appeared on her quilts. Letters and diaries of the period confirm that most women considered the bearing and raising of their children the most important accomplishment of their life. By quilting into her work the outline of her child's hand she was telling us of her greatest glory in the medium she knew best.

It was into that small hand that needle and thread would soon be passed and the cycle of American quilts begun again.

FIGURE 108. *Wild Goose Chase (detail), 1880. See Plate 22. The date appears in the palm of the quilted baby's hand. Maryland. 39¾″ × 37½″. Cotton. Collection of Adrienne and Howard Moss.* Courtesy of Stella Rubin

NOTES

INTRODUCTION

1. Cited by Julia Cherry Spruill, *Women's Life and Work in the Southern Colonies* (New York: W. W. Norton and Company, Inc., 1972), p. 52.

CHAPTER 1

1. Robert H. Baker, *Astronomy* (New Jersey: D. Van Nostrand Company Inc., 1955), p. 334.

2. Described in *The Maryland Gazette* (Baltimore) of September 10, 1790. Cited by Beatrice B. Garvan and Charles F. Hummel, *The Pennyslvania Germans: A Celebration of Their Arts 1683–1850* Philadelphia: Philadelphia Museum of Art, 1982), p. 62.

3. Marion L. Channing, ed., *Laura Russell Remembers* (New Bedford, Mass.: Reynolds-Dewalt Printing, Inc., 1970), p. 31. Miss Russell's manuscript copy, "Old-Time New England," is in the collection of the Pilgrim Society of Plymouth, Massachusetts.

4. Evelyn D. Ward, *The Children of Bladensfield* (New York: Viking Press, 1978), pp. 13–14.

5. Roger Tory Peterson, *The Birds* (New York: Time, Incorporated, 1963), pp. 78, 105–107.

6. Jean Lipton, *Rufus Porter Rediscovered* (New York: The Hudson River Museum, 1980), Plates 9 and 16.

7. Francis Daniel Pastorious, 1684. Cited by Beatrice B. Garvan and Charles F. Hummel, *The Pennsylvania Germans: A Celebration of Their Arts 1683–1850* (Philadelphia: Philadelphia Museum of Art, 1982), p. 37.

8. This rationale for the introduction of botany into a girl's school curriculum was set forth in an article, "Botany for Schools," in the *American Journal of Education* published in 1829. The article may have been written by William Russell, who edited the journal from 1826 to 1829.

9. Peter Coats, *Roses* (London: Octopus Book Limited, 1973), p. 5.

10. Tamsen Donner. Cited by Kenneth L. Homes, ed., *Covered Wagon Women: Diaries and Letters from the Western Trails 1840–1890* (Glendale, Calif.: The Arthur H. Clark Company, 1983), p. 72.

CHAPTER 2

1. Cited by Clifton Johnson, *Old-Time Schools and School-books* (New York: The Macmillan Company, 1904), p. 243.

2. Cited by Elizabeth George Speare, *Child Life in New England: 1790–1840* (Sturbridge, Massachusetts: Old Sturbridge , Inc., 1972), p. 16.

3. Herbert Ridgeway Collins, *Threads of History* (Washington, D.C.: Smithsonian Institution Press, 1979), Figure 60, p. 73.

4. Cited by Johnson, p. 243.

5. Florence F. Pettit, *America's Printed and Painted Fabrics: 1600–1900* (New York: Hastings House, 1970), p. 187.

6. *Ibid.*, Figure 121, p. 186.

7. Katharine Morrison McClinton, *Antiques of American Childhood* (New York: Clarkson N. Potter, Inc., 1970), p. 332.

8. Cited by Anita Schorsch, *Images of Childhood: An Illustrated Social History* (New York: Mayflower Books, Inc., 1979), p. 89.

9. Cited by Antony and Peter Miall, *The Victorian Nursery Book* (New York: Random House, Inc., 1980), p. 84.

10. Evelyn D. Ward, *The Children of Bladensfield* (New York: Viking Press, 1978), p. 93.

11. John Bunyan, *Pilgrim's Progress* (New York: The Macmillan Company, 1913), p. 72.

12. Bernard Wishy, *The Child and The Republic: The Dawn of Modern American Child Nurture* (Philadelphia: University of Pennsylvania Press, 1968), p. 58.

13. Samuel L. Clemens, *The Adventures of Huckleberry Finn* (Cleveland and New York: The World Publishing Company, 1947), pp. 143–145. A painted oilcloth table cover, identical to the one described by Huck Finn, is illustrated in Florence H. Pettit's *America's Printed and Painted Fabrics* (New York: Hastings House, 1970, p. 137.

14. Louisa May Alcott, *Little Women* (New York and Cleveland: The World Publishing Company, 1969), p. 23.

15. *Ibid.*, p. 22.

16. *Ibid.*

17. Harriet Beecher Stowe, *Pictures and Stories from Uncle Tom's Cabin* (Boston: John P. Jewett and Company, 1853), unpaged.

CHAPTER 3

1. Harriet Martineau, *Retrospect of Western Travel*, 1838. Cited by Ralph K. Andrist, ed., et al in *The American Heritage History of the Making of the Nation* (New York: American Heritage Publishing Co., Inc., 1968), p. 163.

2. John H. Clark, "Overland to the Goldfields of California in 1852," *Kansas Historical Quarterly*, XI (1942), p. 236.

3. Alexis de Tocqueville, *Journey to America* (New Haven: Yale University Press, 1960), p. 341.

CHAPTER 4

1. *The Industries of Philadelphia.* Cited in *Philadelphia: Three Centuries of American Art* (Philadelphia: Philadelphia Museum of Art, 1976), p. 378.

2. David Hanks and Page Talbott, "Daniel Pabst: Philadelphia Cabinetmaker," *Philadelphia Museum of Art Bulletin*, vol. 73, no. 316 (Philadelphia: Philadelphia Museum of Art, April 1977), p. 7.

CHAPTER 5

1. Boleslaw Mastai and Marie-Louise D'Otrange, *The Stars and Stripes: The Evolution of the American Flag* (Fort Worth: Amon Carter Museum, 1973), p. 2.

2. Nathaniel Hawthorne, *The Scarlet Letter* (New York: The Modern Library, 1950), pp. 7–8.

3. William Rush Dunton, Jr., *Old Quilts* (Catonsville, Md.: Privately published, 1946), Plate 50, p. 146.

4. *Ibid.*, Plate 36, p. 120.

5. *Ibid.*, Plate 16, p. 76.

6. *Ibid.*, Plate 46, p. 137.

7. Dena S. Katzenberg, *Baltimore Album Quilts* (Baltimore: The Baltimore Museum of Art, 1981), catalog no. 10, p. 89.

8. *Ibid.*, catalog no. 9, p. 87.

9. Edmund B. Sullivan, *Collecting Political Americana* (New York: Crown Publishers, Inc., 1980), p. 143.

10. William Lloyd Garrison, ed., *The Liberator* (Boston), vol. 7., no. 1., January 2, 1837, p. 3. (The issue of separation within slave families is a complicated one. For additional reading: Herbert G. Gutman, *The Black Family in Slavery and Freedom 1750–1925.*)

11. Ibid.

12. Ibid.

CHAPTER 6

1. William Jennings, "Material Progress of Utah," *Utah Historical Quarterly III*, no. 3 (1930), p. 89.

2. Emma Caroll Seegmiller, "Personal Memories of the United Order of Orderville, Utah," (*Utah Historical Quarterly VII*, no. 4 (1939), p. 175.

3. Ibid.

4. Ibid., p. 174.

CHAPTER 7

1. For the definitive study of needlework tools, see Gay Ann Rogers, *An Illustrated History of Needlework Tools* (London: John Murray [Publishers] Ltd., 1983).

2. Anna Green Winslow, *Diary*. Alice Morse Earle, ed. (Boston: Houghton Mifflin Co., 1899).

3. Mary Andere, *Old Needlework Boxes and Tools* (Newton Abbot, U.K.: David and Charles, 1971), p. 67.

BIBLIOGRAPHY

◆◆◆

Alcott, Louisa May. *Little Women*. New York and Cleveland: The World Publishing Company, 1969.

Allen, Edward B. *Early American Wall Paintings 1710–1850*. Watkins Glen, N. Y.: Century House, 1969.

American Heritage, eds. *Great Days of the Circus*. New York: American Heritage Publishing Co., Inc., 1962.

Andere, Mary. *Old Needlework Boxes and Tools*. Newton Abbot (U.K.): David and Charles, 1971.

Andrist, Ralph K., ed., et al. *The American Heritage History of the Making of the Nation*. New York: American Heritage Publishing Co., Inc., 1968.

Baker, Robert H. *Astronomy*. New Jersey: D. Van Nostrand Company Inc., 1955.

Baugh, Albert C., ed. *A Literary History of England*. New York: Appleton-Century-Crofts Inc., 1948.

Bealer, Alex W., and Ellis, John O. *The Log Cabin: Homes of the American Wilderness*. Barre, Mass.: Barr Publishing, 1979.

Beer, Alice Baldwin. *Trade Goods*. Washington, D.C.: Smithsonian Institution Press, 1970.

Blond, Georges. *The Great Migrations*. New York: Collier Books, 1962.

Brant, Sandra, and Cullman, Elissa. *Small Folks: A Celebration of Childhood in America*. New York: E. P. Dutton, 1980.

Bunyan, John. *Pilgrim's Progress*. New York: The Macmillan Company, 1913.

Butterfield, Roger: *The American Past*. New York: Simon and Schuster, 1976.

Carson, Gerald. *Rum and Reform in Old New England*. Sturbridge, Mass.: Old Sturbridge, Inc., 1976.

Channing, Marion L., ed. *Laura Russell Remembers*. New Bedford, Mass.: Reynolds-DeWalt Printing, Inc., 1970.

Chindahl, George L. *A History of the Circus in America*. Caldwell, Idaho: The Caxton Printers Ltd., 1959.

Clark, John H. "Overland to the Goldfields of California in 1852," *Kansas Historical Quarterly, XI*. 1942.

Clemens, Samuel L. *The Adventures of Huckleberry Finn*. Cleveland and New York: The World Publishing Company, 1947.

Coats, Peter. *Roses*. London: Octopus Books Limited, 1973.

Collins, Herbert Ridgeway. *Threads of History*. Washington, D.C.: Smithsonian Institution Press, 1979.

Dunaway, Philip, and Evans, Mel, eds. *A Treasury of the World's Great Diaries*. New York: Doubleday, 1957.

Dunton, William Rush, Jr. *Old Quilts*. Catonsville, Md.: privately published, 1946.

Fox, Sandi. *Quilts in Utah: A Reflection of the Western Experience*. Exhibition catalog. Salt Lake City: Salt Lake Art Center, 1981.

Garrison, William Lloyd, ed. *The Liberator* (Boston). vol 7., no. 1. January 2, 1837.

Garvan, Beatrice B., and Hummel, Charles F. *The Pennsylvania Germans: A Celebration of Their Arts 1683–1850*. Exhibition catalog. Philadelphia: Philadelphia Museum of Art, 1982.

Gehret, Ellen J., and Keyser, Alan G. *The Homespun Textile Tradition of the Pennsylvania Germans*. Exhibition catalog. Harrisburg: Pennsylvania Historical and Museum Commission, 1976.

Gilbert, Russell Wieder. *A Picture of the Pennsylvania Germans*. Gettysburg: The Pennsylvania Historical Association, 1971.

Green, Harvey. *The Light of the Home: An Intimate View of the Lives of Women in Victorian America*. New York: Pantheon Books, 1983.

Gutman, Herbert G. *The Black Family in Slavery and Freedom: 1750–1925*. New York: Vintage Books, 1977.

Harris, Joel Chandler. *Uncle Remus, His Songs and His Sayings, the Folk-Lore of the Old Plantation*. New York: D. Appleton and Co., 1881.

Haviland, Virginia, and Coughlan, Margaret N., eds. *Yankee Doodle's Literary Sampler of Prose, Poetry and Pictures*. New York: Thomas Y. Crowell Company, 1974.

Hawgood, John A. *America's Western Frontiers*. New York: Alfred A. Knopf, 1967.

Hawthorne, Nathaniel. *The Scarlet Letter*. New York: Modern Library, 1950.

Hazen, Edward. *The Panorama of Professions and Trades*. Philadelphia: Uriah Hunt, 1837.

Heinroth, Oskar and Katharina. *The Birds*. London: Faber and Faber, 1959.

Holmes, Kenneth L., ed. *Covered Wagon Women: Diaries and Letters from the Western Trails 1840–1890*, vol. 1. Glendale, Calif.: The Arthur H. Clark Company, 1983.

Horwitz, Elinor Lander. *The Bird, the Banner, and Uncle Sam: Images of America in Folk and Popular Art*. Philadelphia and New York: J. B. Lippincott Company, 1976.

Hostetler, John A. *Amish Society*. Baltimore: The John Hopkins University Press, 1981.

James, Philip. *Children's Books of Yesterday*. New York: Studio Publications Inc., 1933.

Jennings, William. "Material Progress of Utah." *Utah Historical Quarterly III:* no. 3, 1930.

Johnson, Clifton. *Old-Time Schools and School-books*. New York: The Macmillan Company, 1904.

Katzenberg. Dena S. *Baltimore Album Quilts*. Exhibition catalog. Baltimore: The Baltimore Museum of Art, 1981.

Lichten, Frances. *Folk Arat of Rural Pennsylvania*. New York: Charles Scribner's Sons, 1946.

Life, eds. *America's Arts and Skills*. New York: E. P. Dutton and Co., Inc., 1957.

Lipton, Jean. *Rufus Porter Rediscovered*. Exhibition catalog. New York: The Hudson River Museum, 1980.

McClinton, Katharine Morrison. *Antiques of American Childhood*. New York: Clarkson N. Potter, Inc., 1970.

Mastai, Boleslaw, and D'Otrange, Marie Louise. *The Stars and Stripes: The Evolution of the American Flag*. Fort Worth: Amon Carter Museum, 1973.

Melder, Keith E. *The Village and the Nation*. Sturbridge, Mass.: Old Sturbridge, Inc., 1976.

Miall, Antony and Peter. *The Victorian Nursery Book*. New York: Random House, Inc., 1980.

Montgomery, Florence. *Printed Textiles: English and American Cottons and Linens, 1700–1850*. New York: The Viking Press, 1969.

Parrington, Vernon Louis. *Main Currents in American Thought*. New York: Harcourt, Brace and Company, 1930.

Peterson, Roger Tory. *The Birds*. New York: Time Incorporated, 1963.

Pettit, Florence H. *America's Indigo Blues: Resist-printed and Dyed Textiles of the Eighteenth Century*. New York: Hastings House, 1974.

———. *America's Printed and Painted Fabrics: 1600–1900*. New York: Hastings House, 1970.

Philadelphia Museum of Art. *Philadelphia: Three Centuries of American Art*. Exhibition catalog. Philadelphia: Philadelphia Museum of Art, 1976.

Rogers, Gay Ann. *An Illustrated History of Needlework Tools*. London: John Murray (Publishers) Ltd., 1983.

Schorsch, Anita. *Images of Childhood: An Illustrated Social History*. New York: Mayflower Books, Inc., 1979.

Seegmiller, Emma Caroll. "Personal Memories of the United Order of Orderville, Utah." *Utah Historical Quarterly VII*: no. 4, 1939.

Speare, Elizabeth George. *Child Life in New England, 1790–1840.* Sturbridge, Mass.: Old Sturbridge Inc., 1961.

Spruill, Julia Cherry. *Women's Life and Work in the Southern Colonies.* New York: W. W. Norton and Company, Inc., 1972.

Stowe, Harriet Beecher. *Pictures and Stories from Uncle Tom's Cabin.* Boston: John P. Jewett and Company, 1853.

———. *Uncle Tom's Cabin.* Boston and New York: Houghton Mifflin Company, 1894.

Sullivan, Edmund B. *Collecting Political Americana.* New York: Crown Publishers, Inc., 1980.

Swan, Susan Burrows. *Plain & Fancy: American Women and Their Needlework 1700–1850.* New York: Holt, Rinehart and Winston, 1977.

Tracy, Berry B., et al. *19th-Century America: Furniture and Other Decorative Arts.* Exhibition catalog. New York: The Metropolitan Museum of Art, 1970.

Turner, Frederick Jackson. *The Frontier in American History.* New York: Henry Holt and Company, 1920.

Ward, Evelyn D. *The Children of Bladensfield.* New York: Viking Press, 1978.

Waring, Janet. *Early American Stencils on Walls and Furniture.* Watkins Glen, N. Y.: Century House, 1968.

Weslager, Clinton A. *The Log Cabin in America.* New Brunswick: Rutgers University Press, 1969.

Winslow, Anna Green. *Diary.* Edited by Alice Morse Earle. Boston: Houghton Mifflin Company, 1899.

Wishy, Bernard. *The Child and the Republic: The Dawn of American Child Nurture.* Philadelphia: University of Pennyslvania Press, 1968.

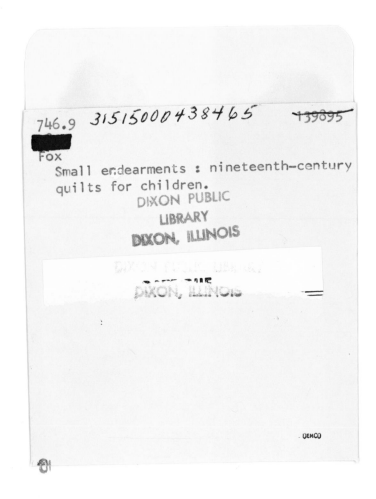